ORTHODOXY
a modern translation

By G.K. Chesterton

Edited by Peter Northcutt

modernsaints

modernsaints.com
Copyright © 2021 Peter Northcutt
All rights reserved.
ISBN: 9798378206728

 modernsaints

The most important Christian books made modern.

It's time we meet our ancestors.
Go to modernsaints.com or follow
@WeAreModernSaints.

CONTENTS

PREFACE

If you were to travel back in time one hundred years to observe an ordinary day on London's famous Fleet Street, your eye would soon be caught by a particularly jolly journalist named G.K. Chesterton. At first, you wouldn't fully appreciate the object of your observation. You wouldn't think this man would one day be called a saint too good for this world, or a prophet of common sense calling out from the intellectual wilderness, or a happy-hearted boy who got stuck in the body of a giant genius. You wouldn't assume his writing would be praised by the likes of Ernest Hemingway, Neil Gaiman, and Orson Welles. You would, however, quickly see that this man was simply larger than life–in more ways than one.

The first thing you would notice about this giant would be his literal largeness. Standing six foot four and weighing nearly three hundred pounds, his enormous figure stood out among the London crowds. In fact, he often bragged about being the most polite man in England, because on a bus he could offer his seat to not just one but three ladies at once.

After noticing his considerable size, you would then notice his dress. With a cigar poking through his mustache and glasses on the end of his nose, he paraded the streets donning a cape on his back, a swordstick in his hand, and a crumpled hat fit snugly over his disheveled hair. It would seem to you as if he had just jaunted out of one of his own whimsical story books.

Chesterton was, indeed, famous for his gigantic imagination and for often getting lost in it. If, after spotting him in the street, you were to follow him to the train station, you might see him sit and watch as the trains rushed past each other, pretending they were knights in a joust, never realizing he missed the train he needed to catch. Chesterton relied on his wife to keep track of his appointments, and on one particular evening he sent a helpless message to her, writing, "Am at Market Harborough. Where ought I to be?" "Home," she replied.

If you were to introduce yourself, however, Chesterton would become immensely present. Though he quickly became an English celebrity, he never lacked time for people, especially children. Once, after a child returned home from a birthday party at the Chesterton house, her parents asked if G.K. said anything profound or witty. The child replied, "I don't know about that, but you should see Mr. Chesterton catch buns in his mouth!"

The largest thing about him, however, may have been his profound and witty words. Chesterton was, first and foremost, a writer. Marked by wonder, wit, joy, and paradox, his words immerse you in an experience difficult to describe. As Chesterton himself often uses illustrations to make his points, I will do the same.

When you read his words, it feels as if you've stepped into a roller coaster. (I would apologize for the juvenile nature of the illustration, but Chesterton wouldn't consider "juvenile" a pejorative.) In *Orthodoxy*, for example, he bursts out the gate with an imaginative illustration, knocking your head back in astonishment from the force of it. He then uses that illustration to make a point you've never considered but seems so obvious. This sensation feels as if he has turned you upside down. He shows you the world you've always known, but from a new angle.

He then whips you around corners, shifting violently from topic to topic. He jerks you one way, then the other—then, just when you question where he's taking you, he whips you back to the center, tying everything together. It's only then that you realize every inch of unpredictable track you traveled was necessary for the thrill he intended you to feel.

The most memorable parts of this ride, however, are when you chug along, gaining speed, getting faster and faster. You are getting comfortable, becoming acclimated to the twists and turns, when you find yourself flying face first into the seat in front of you. The car comes to a screeching halt in the middle of the track as you take out your highlighter and circle a one-liner you never saw coming, one that you vow to remember forever.

This mind-bending style of writing led Chesterton to become one of the most beloved and prolific writers of the twentieth century. He wrote over a hundred books, one of which, called *The Everlasting Man,* helped lead a young C.S. Lewis to Christianity. He wrote roughly two hundred short stories, including a detective series about a charming, crime-fighting priest called Father Brown, which can now be found on Netflix. He wrote five novels, including *The Napoleon of Notting Hill,* which inspired Michael Collins to lead a movement for Irish Independence and, perhaps, inspired George Orwell's *1984.* He penned hundreds of poems, moving T.S. Eliot to assert that Chesterton "deserves a permanent claim on our loyalty." What Chesterton loved most, however, was the essay. He wrote over four thousand newspaper essays for London publishers about anything and everything—from religion and politics to cheese and the contents of his own overstuffed pockets. And, to top it off, one of these essays written in the *Illustrated London News* inspired Mahatma Gandhi to lead the movement for Indian independence.

I have yet to mention, however, what you hold in your hands now. *Orthodoxy*–a book that author Philip Yancey said "had as much influence on (his) spiritual direction as any single book"–could be his most important work. This top-ten Christian classic recounts the process of how Chesterton himself grew from an atheist to a Christian and of how the ancient faith can cure a modern world gone mad. *Orthodoxy* is no ordinary book of apologetics, however, because it primarily focuses not on whether Christianity is objectively true, but whether it is the most adventurous and healthy way to live. Chesterton compares the faith to other popular trends of thought, then shows that, of all the religions and philosophies available, Christianity best satisfies our deepest spiritual need–the need for a life of romance.

This book isn't a prosaic theological treatise so much as poetic pop-philosophy. It doesn't try to build the most foolproof arguments, but instead tries to paint the most beautiful pictures. For the non-Christian, *Orthodoxy* may paint the first attractive picture of Christianity you have seen, opening the door for further spiritual exploration. For the Christian, it will help you make sense of the modern world, restore the fun in your faith, and remind you that the story of Jesus is not only true, but something you *want* to be true, which, on your days of doubt, may draw you back to God better than any logical argument.

Chesterton didn't predict that *Orthodoxy* would have the impact it did (which, ironically, turned out to be one of the only things he didn't predict correctly). In his elephantine humility, he sold the book to his publisher for a hundred pounds. He did not know readers would devour it for centuries to come and that it would serve as almost a prophecy of our current, postmodern society. But this humility which makes *Orthodoxy* such a wonderful read is also what makes it so difficult.

Chesterton didn't predict the longevity of his work, so the book is filled to the brim with references only twentieth-century Londoners would understand. To his credit, the masses loved this because he often connected his points to popular people or places. He did not consider, however, that no one would know these people and places a hundred years later. These antiquated references combined with an outdated vocabulary and verbiage leave modern readers feeling it isn't worth it to wade through the book with an encyclopedia in one hand and a dictionary in the other.

This modern translation was written to break down those unnecessary walls between us and Chesterton. Here are the four basic ways in which this book was adapted:

- Obscure references were either explained within the text or else removed entirely if not integral to the argument,
- Sentence structures and vocabulary were updated to better suit modern readers,
- Sub-headings were added to help readers follow the flow of Chesterton's unique arguments,
- And, paragraphs were broken into smaller chunks for ease of reading.

The result of these adaptations is a fun and fresh reading experience void of needless struggle–both fully Chesterton and fully enjoyable.

So, I look forward to the many emails from newcomers to the Chesterton fan club. I will read about how you now feel the world is enchanted and full of meaning, or about how you now see the madness of materialism, or about how you are no longer an optimist or a pessimist but instead a cosmic patriot. There are a thousand lessons to be learned and a thousand more puns to be enjoyed, but whatever you gain, I hope you share it with me and with others.

I will add one more note here. Chesterton calls chapters two and three "the most boring business of this book." These chapters focus not on his own ideas but on those of his peers. My suggestion, if you happen to agree with his opinion, is to skip to chapter four, "The Ethics of Elfland." Here Chesterton begins painting his own view of the world and it is as enchanting as it sounds. Without exaggeration, it may change the way you see everything.

Happy reading, and may your faith be refreshed.

–Peter Northcutt

1

Introduction in Defense of Everything Else

My only possible excuse for writing this book is that I was challenged to do it. After all, even a bad shot is dignified when he accepts a duel.

The challenge came from several of my critics whose intelligence I highly respect. They said I tend to criticize other people's ideas without explaining or supporting my own. "I'll start to worry about my philosophy," one of them said, "when Mr. Chesterton has given us his." That may have been a reckless thing to say to a person who is always too eager to write books.

If my critics read this book, they will find that I have tried–in a vague and personal way, in a collection of mental images rather than in a series of logical deductions–to explain the philosophy I have come to believe. I won't call it *my* philosophy, because I didn't make it. God and humanity made it. And it made me.

Romance: Our Two-Sided Spiritual Need

I have often wanted to write a story about an English explorer who sailed slightly off course and accidentally re-discovered England, believing it was a new island in the South Pacific. I always find, however, that I am either too busy or too lazy to write this delightful story, so I may as well give it away here as an illustration.

Armed to the teeth, our hero landed, planting the British flag on what he thought was barbaric soil but later learned was only the coast of England. You are probably thinking now that our hero felt like a fool. I am not going to say he didn't look like one, but if you think he *felt* like a fool, or that foolishness was at least what he felt most, then you don't understand the rich romantic nature of the hero of this tale. His mistake was, actually, very lucky. And he knew it was lucky, if he is the man I think he is.

What could be better than to have, within the same few minutes, all the heart-pounding terror of exploring combined with all the peace and security of coming home again? What could be better than having all the fun of discovering South Africa without the terrible need of actually landing there? What could be more glorious than to brace yourself to survive in New South Wales, and then realize with a gush of happy tears that it was really old South Wales all along? This, to me, seems to be the main question for philosophers, and is, in a way, the main question of this book. How can we seem to be surprised by this world and yet also feel at home in it? How can this odd, universal city—with all its many-legged citizens, with its monstrous and magical lamps—how can this world give us, at the same time, the fascination of a foreign town as well as the comfort and confidence of our own town?

To prove that a faith or a philosophy is true from every angle would be too big of a project, even for a much bigger book than this. Instead, I will follow this one train of thought: I want to show that my Christian faith answers our two-sided spiritual need—the need for this mixture of the familiar and the unfamiliar. Christian tradition correctly calls this mixture "romance," because the word itself carries the mystery and ancient meaning of Rome.

Now, we know that anyone trying to argue anything should always begin by stating what they are *not* trying to argue. When stating what they propose to prove, they should always state what they do *not* propose to prove. The thing I am not trying to prove in this book, the thing I will assume is common ground between myself and any average reader, is this desire for an active and imaginative life, picturesque and full of poetical curiosity. If someone says that death is better than life, or a boring life is better than variety and adventure, then they are not one of the ordinary people I am writing to. If a person prefers nothing, I can give them nothing.

Nearly all the people I have met, however, would agree to the general idea that we need this life of practical romance—the combination of something strange with something secure. We need a view of the world that combines the idea of wonder and the idea of welcome. We need to be happy in this wonderland without ever being simply comfortable. It is *this* train of thought, *this* great quality of my faith, that I will primarily explore in this book.

The Fool of This Story

I have an interesting reason for mentioning our explorer who discovered England. Because, you see, I am that explorer. I discovered England. I can't see how this book can avoid being self-centered, and to be honest, I'm not sure how it can avoid being boring. However, if it turns out to be dull, it might save me from the criticism I fear most: being accused of flippancy, of not taking things seriously.

A clever, deceptive argument just for the sake of argument is the one thing I despise the most, and ironically, it's the accusation I often face. I don't know anything as disgusting as a mere paradox, a pointless word puzzle, a brilliant defense of the indefensible. If it were true, as some say, that Mr. George Bernard Shaw thrives on paradox, then he would be a common millionaire. With his mental ability, he could come up with one of these deceptions every six minutes–it's as easy as lying, because essentially, it *is* lying.

But the truth is, Mr. Shaw is cruelly crippled by the fact that he can't tell a lie unless he genuinely believes it's the truth. I find myself in the same intolerable predicament. I've never said anything just for the sake of being funny; though, of course, I've had the typical human vanity and might have found something funny because I said it. Describing an encounter with a mythical creature like a gorgon or a griffin is one thing, but discovering that a rhinoceros actually does exist and taking pleasure in the fact that it looks like it shouldn't is another. I seek the truth, but it's possible that I instinctively pursue the more extraordinary truths. So, I present this book with the kindest regards to all the lovely people who hate what I write, and who think of it (for good reason, maybe) as a poor prank or a single tiresome joke.

If this book is a joke, however, it is a joke against me. I am the man who, with incredible fearlessness, discovered what had been discovered before. If there is even a hint of absurdity in the following pages, then the absurdity is at my own expense. This book explains how I was so proud to be the first person to set foot in England, and then I realized I was the last. It tells stories of my elephantine adventures in search of what is so obvious to so many. No one can think my journey

---

◉ The Glittering Sword ◉

A book titled "Orthodoxy" may not immediately suggest laugh-out-loud humor, but, unexpectedly, Chesterton's exploration of serious topics carries a comedic touch. In asserting that a thing can be both humorous *and* true, he fervently rejected the notion that funny and serious are opposites, stating, "Funny is the opposite of not funny, and nothing else." Rather than deploying humor merely for amusement, Chesterton strategically uses it to circumvent the mental defenses of his readers, noting that "humor can get in under the door while seriousness is still fumbling at the handle." C.S. Lewis, drawn to Chesterton's unique blend of humor and argument, had this to say:

"I did not need to accept what Chesterton said in order to enjoy it. His humor was of the kind which I like best – not 'jokes' imbedded in the page like currants in a cake... but the humor which is not in any way separable from the argument. The sword glitters not because the swordsman set out to make it glitter but because he is fighting for his life and therefore moving it very quickly."

---

more ridiculous than I already do. No reader can accuse me of making a fool of them. I am the fool of this story, and no rebel shall hurl me from my throne.

I freely admit all the idiotic ambitions of my past. Like all other serious little boys, I tried to be ten minutes ahead of the curve, and then I found I was eighteen hundred years behind it. I proclaimed the truths I found with an embarrassing amount of arrogance, and though I have held on to these truths, I was punished in the most fitting way–I discovered, not that they weren't truths, but that they weren't *mine*. When I thought I stood alone, I was really in the ridiculous position of being backed by all of Christian theology. It may have been, God forgive me, that I did try to be original. But what I really did was invent, all on my own, a lesser version of what religious tradition already created. The explorer thought he was the first to find England; I thought I was the first to find *Europe*. I tried to find a nice, unorthodox belief of my own, and when I had put the last touches on it, I discovered that it was orthodoxy.

I hope this account of my happy fiasco entertains someone. It might amuse a friend (or an enemy) to read about how I gradually learned the truth from the wisdom of random legends or the errors of major philosophies, when I could have learned it in my Sunday School material, if I had ever read it. It may or may not be entertaining to read about what I found in a political rally or a foreign temple, when I could have found it in the nearest church. If anyone is entertained by learning how the flowers of the field, or the ads on a bus, or the accidents of politics, or the growing pains of youth all came together in a certain order to create in me a certain conviction of Christian orthodoxy, then he just might read this book. But it would only be fair to divide the labor here. I have written this book, and nothing on earth could convince me to read it.

The Best Foundation

I will add one small note which comes at the beginning of the book, as a note should. The word "orthodoxy" refers to what we call the Apostles' Creed, a statement of foundational Christian beliefs that everyone calling themselves a Christian would agree on until just a short time ago, as well as the general conduct of those throughout history who held to this creed. So, this book discusses only the fact that the *central* Christian theology (which is sufficiently summarized in the Apostles' Creed) is the best source of energy and sound ethics.

These limited number of pages force me to focus only on what I have gotten from this creed. I won't discuss the things most argued about among modern Christians, including the question of how we ourselves got it. This isn't a systematic history of the church but instead a sort of disordered autobiography. But if anyone wants my opinion about the authoritative nature of this creed, they need only to throw me another challenge, and I will write them another book.

2

The Maniac

Thoroughly worldly people often struggle to comprehend even the world. Instead, they simply repeat a few cynical expressions that are not true.

I remember walking with a successful publisher once, and he said something which I had heard several times before and is almost a motto for the modern world. But I had heard it one too many times, and when he said it, I suddenly realized there was no truth in it. The publisher said of somebody, "That man will be alright; he believes in himself." And I remember that as I lifted my head to listen, a sign that said "Hanwell" (a town known for its insane asylum) caught my eye.

I said to him, "Would you like to know where those who really believe in themselves live? I can tell you. I know of people who believe in themselves more extremely than Napoleon or Caesar. I know where to find these undying stars of certainty and success. I can guide you to the thrones of these Supermen. The people who really believe in themselves are all in insane asylums."

He replied mildly that, actually, there were many who believed in themselves that were *not* in insane asylums.

"Yes, there are," I said. "And you of all people should know them. You work in the publishing industry. That drunken poet who couldn't write poetry, she believed in herself. That old preacher with the long epic who you were hiding from in a back room, he believed in himself. If you would consider your business experience instead of your ugly philosophy of self-reliance, you would know that believing in oneself is one of the most common signs of a loon.

"Actors who can't act believe in themselves, and debtors who won't pay their debts. Instead of saying people will succeed because they believe in themselves, it would be much more accurate to say they will fail. Complete self-confidence isn't just a sin; complete self-confidence is a *weakness*. Completely believing in oneself is idiotic and superstitious. The man who believes in himself has 'Hanwell' written on his forehead as plain as it is written on that sign."

And to everything I said, my publisher friend gave a very deep reply that affected me. He said, "Well, if people shouldn't believe in themselves, what should they believe in?"

After a long pause, I replied, "I'll go home and write a book to answer that question." This is the book I have written.

Let Us Start at the Madhouse

I think this book may as well start where our discussion started—in the neighborhood of the madhouse. Modern scientists feel the need to begin all their questions and studies with a solid fact. The ancient religious thinkers also felt that need. So, they began with the existence of sin–a fact as practical as potatoes. Some people may have doubted whether they could be washed in miraculous waters. No one ever doubted, however, that they wanted to be washed.

Lately, however, even our religious leaders have started to deny this first fact of sin: not the existence of the highly-questioned waters, but the existence of the unquestionable dirt. These new theologians dispute original sin, which is the only part of Christian theology that can actually be proven. Many people believe in the sinlessness of God, which they can't see or comprehend even in their dreams. But some also deny the sinfulness of humans, which they can see every day in the street.

Everyone–the strongest saints and the strongest skeptics–used to start their argument with the existence of evil. If it is true (and it is) that a man can feel perfectly happy when skinning a cat, then religious philosophers can only draw one of two conclusions. They must either deny the existence of God, which all atheists do, or they must deny the present union of God and man, as all Christians do. The new theologian seems to think the most rational solution is to deny the dead cat.

So, we find ourselves in a remarkable situation in which we can't (if we want to appeal to everyone) start our argument where our ancestors did, with the fact of sin. The fact of sin was clear as day to them (and to me), but this fact has now been watered down or denied. But while modern people deny the existence of sin, I don't think they have quite yet denied the existence of the insane asylum. We can all agree that people's brains can go bad just as obviously as moldy bread. People deny Hell, but at least they don't deny Hanwell. At least not yet. So, for the purpose of my main argument, we will replace Hell with Hanwell. This is what I mean: all thoughts and theories were once judged by whether they tended to make a person lose their soul, but, for our purpose today, we will judge these thoughts and theories by whether they tend to make a person lose their *mind.*

The Ugliness of Insanity

Now, some people speak lightly of insanity, as if it is somehow an attractive thing to be insane. But if you think about it, whenever a disease seems beautiful, it is generally someone else's disease. A blind man may be picturesque, but it requires two working eyes of your own to see the picture. And similarly, the wildest, most insane poetry can only be enjoyed by the sane. The insane person sees no poetry in insanity because they think it is just another ordinary, boring thing. A man who thinks he is a chicken considers himself as ordinary as a chicken. A woman who thinks she is a piece of glass considers herself as dull as a piece of glass. It is this kind of one-track brain that makes them both boring and insane. We only think they are amusing because we see the irony of their idea, and it is only because they don't see the irony of their idea that they are locked up in the asylum at all.

In short, odd things only strike ordinary people as odd. Odd things don't strike odd people. This is why sane people have much more fun while insane people always complain about the boredom of life. This also explains why new novels die so quickly, and why the old fairy tales will live forever. The old fairy tale makes the hero a normal human boy; it is his adventures that are amazing, and they amaze him *because* he is normal. But in the average modern novel, the hero is abnormal. The center of the story is not centrally balanced. As a result, the wildest adventures fail to affect him enough, and the book becomes boring. You can make a story out of a boy living with dragons, but not out of a dragon living with dragons. The fairy tale describes what a normal person will do in a wild world. The dark realistic novel of today describes what a lunatic will do in a boring world.

What Makes a Man Lose His Mind?

We have begun our intellectual journey with the madhouse, that evil and fantastic inn. Now, if we are to address the idea of mental sanity, the first thing we should do is to dismiss one big and common mistake. There is an idea floating around that imagination, especially spiritual imagination, is dangerous to mental health. Most people think poets are psychologically unstable. But facts and history just don't agree. Most of the great poets have not only been sane, but extremely business-like. And if a young Shakespeare really did care for the horses at the theater, it's because he was the most responsible man for the job.

Imagination does not produce insanity. What *does* produce insanity is reason. Poets don't go mad, but chess players do. Mathematicians go mad, and cashiers, but creative artists almost never. I am not, as you will find, attacking logic at all. I am only saying the danger of insanity is found in logic, not in imagination. Creating art is as good and healthy as creating a child.

 Brushed Aside

If you've reached this point in the book, you might have formed the impression that Chesterton was destined to be a writer. But surprisingly, his early ambitions led him to art school. It was during his time at the Slade School of Art in London that he crossed paths with his future wife. To fund an engagement ring, he began writing book reviews for newspapers. Although he eventually abandoned his artistic dreams to embark on a burgeoning writing career, Chesterton had genuine talent and illustrated several books throughout his lifetime. Interestingly, he's not the only Christian writer known for his illustrations; literary luminaries like C.S. Lewis and J.R.R. Tolkien were also known to dabble in doodling.

We should also note that when a poet really was unhealthy, it was usually because he had a weak spot of reasonable thinking on his brain. Edgar Allan Poe, for example, really was unhealthy–not because he was lost in his own imagination, but because he was especially analytical. Even chess was too imaginative and creative. He disliked chess because it was full of knights and castles, like a poem. He openly preferred the black pieces of checkers because they were more like simple dots on a graph. But this is maybe the strongest example: only one great English poet, William Cowper, went crazy. And he was driven crazy by logic, by the ugly and unusual logic of predestination. Poetry wasn't the disease, it was the medicine; poetry was what kept him alive.

We see everywhere that men don't go insane by dreaming. Art critics are much crazier than artists. Homer is calm and collected; it is his critics who tear him to pieces like dogs. Shakespeare knows himself; it is only some of his critics who have discovered that he was somebody else. And even though John, the writer of Revelation, saw many strange monsters in that dream-like vision, he didn't see any creature so wild as one of his own commentators.

My point here is simple. Poetry is sane because it happily floats along in an infinite ocean; reason attempts to cross that infinite ocean, trying to make it somehow finite. The result is mental exhaustion. To take everything in is a nice exercise, but to understand everything is a heavy strain. The poet only desires a place in which to praise, an expansive world to stretch himself in. The poet only asks to get his head into the heavens. It is the logical thinker who seeks to get the heavens into his head. And it is *his* head that splits.

I think it is relevant to point out here that people usually support this astonishing mistake with a famous quote, a quote that happens to be astonishingly misquoted. We have all heard people quote the poet John Dryden as saying, "Great genius is to madness near allied." But Dryden didn't say that great genius was to madness near allied. Dryden actually was a great genius, and he knew better. Dryden was one of the most sensible people of his age, and also happened to be one of the most romantic. What Dryden actually said was, "Great wits (or intelligence) is to madness near allied." And he was right about that. Intelligence and genius are not the same thing. It is the rapid rate of the brain that creates the danger of a breakdown.

People should also remember what sort of man Dryden was talking about when he said this. He wasn't talking about great visionary poets like Henry Vaughan or George Herbert. He was talking about the dark, cynical men of the world—skeptics, diplomats, and powerful politicians. These men are indeed allies with madness. They constantly weigh their own brains against others, and that is a dangerous game to play. It is always dangerous for the brain to think of itself. You may ask why we use the phrase, "As mad as a hatter." A less serious person than me might say a hat maker is mad because he must measure the human head.

Arguing with a Madman

If great, logical thinkers are often maniacal and insane, then it must also be true that maniacs are usually great thinkers. I remember once I debated a gifted writer named R.B. Suthers about the idea of free will. Suthers said that free will was lunacy because it meant actions without a cause, and only the actions of lunatics would be without cause. I won't dwell here on this disastrous error in determinist logic. It should be obvious that if any actions, even the actions of an insane person, can be without cause, then that is the end of determinism. If the chain of cause and effect (which is the main principle of determinism) can be broken for a madman, then it can be broken for any man.

The point here is that Mr. Suthers evidently doesn't know anything about lunatics. The one thing you can't say about a lunatic is that his actions are causeless. If any human action could be called at all causeless, it would be the small acts of a healthy man: whistling as he walks, swiping at the grass with a stick, clicking his heels or rubbing his hands. It is the happy, balanced person that does the useless things. The sick person isn't healthy enough to be idle.

The madman could never even understand the careless and causeless actions of the healthy man, because the madman (like the determinist) usually sees too much cause in eve-rything. He would see every little activity around him as a conspiracy against him. He would think that a man mowing his yard was an attack on private property. He would think a man clicking his heels was a signal to a secret accomplice. If the madman could become careless about these insignificant things if only for a second, he would become sane.

Anyone who has had the bad luck of talking with some-one in the heart or on the edge of mental disorder knows that their most sinister quality is a great attention to detail; they connect things together in a map more elaborate than a maze. If you argue with a madman, it is more than likely you will lose that argument. In many ways his brain operates faster be-cause it isn't bogged down by the mental operations that come with having a healthy mind. He isn't hampered by a sense of humor or by love or by simple, common experiences. He is actually *more* logical for losing some of his mental health. And because of this, the common phrase used to de-scribe insanity is a misleading one in this case. The madman isn't the man who has lost his ability to think. The madman is the man who has lost everything *except* his ability to think.

When a madman explains something, his thinking is al-ways complete and well-structured from a logical point of view. We could also say that the insane man's explanation, if not correct and conclusive, is at least unable to be disproven successfully. We can observe this in two or three of the most common kinds of madness. For example, if a man says that there is a conspiracy against him, the only way to dispute this is to tell him that everyone denies they are conspirators, which is exactly what conspirators would do. His explana-tion is just as good as ours. Or if a man claims he is the rightful

King of England, it is not a complete answer to say the current authorities call him crazy. Because if he really were the King of England, that might be the wisest thing for the current authorities to do. Or if a man says that he is Jesus Christ, there is no use telling him the world denies his godliness. After all, the world denied Christ's.

Nevertheless, he is wrong. But if we try to retrace his argument and find where he went wrong, we might not find it quite as easily as expected. Maybe the best way to explain him is to say this: his mind moves in a perfect but tiny circle. A small circle is just as infinitely round as a large circle; but even though it is just as infinite, it is not as large. In the same way, the insane man's explanation is just as complete as the sane man's, but it is not as large. A bullet is as round as the world, but it isn't the world. There is such a thing as a small and cramped eternity; you might see this in many modern religions.

Curing a Madman

If I may make an observation, it seems the strongest and most unmistakable sign of madness is this combination of two things: complete logic and spiritual shrinkage. The lunatic's theory explains a large number of things, but it doesn't explain them in a large way. To put it differently, if you were dealing with a brain that was growing sick, your first concern wouldn't be to give it more arguments to think about, but instead to give it air to breathe, to convince it there was something cleaner and cooler outside the suffocating stuffiness of a single argument.

Let's take, for example, the first case that I said was typical of madness, the man who accused everybody of conspiring against him. If we could express to him our deepest feelings, trying our best to dissuade him from his obsession, I think we would say something like this:

Oh, I admit you really do believe this conspiracy theory is true, and that it actually does explain several things. I admit your explanation explains quite a lot. But look at everything it leaves out! Is your story the only story in the world? Is everyone busy with your business?

Let's say you're right about some details of your theory. Maybe when the man in the street didn't seem to see you it was only because he was very sneaky. And maybe when the policeman asked you your name, he really did know it already. But how much happier would you be if you only knew these people cared nothing about you! How much larger your life would be if you could become smaller in it, if you could be honestly curious about the lives of other people, if you could see them walking as they really are in all their sunny selfishness and their vibrant indifference to you!

You would find yourself interested in them, because they weren't interested in you. You would break out of this tiny and tacky theater where you play out your own little story over and over, and you would find yourself under a freer sky in a street full of spectacular strangers.

Or let's take the second case of madness of the man who claims he is King. Your first instinct would be to answer,

Alright, so maybe you know you are the King of England. But why would you accept the crown? If you wanted, you could be a normal human and look down on all the kings of the earth.

Or it might be the third case of the man who called himself Christ. If we said what we felt, we would say,

So, you are the Creator and Redeemer of the world. But what a small world this must be! What a little heaven you must dwell in, with angels no bigger than butterflies! How sad it must be to be God, especially such a puny God! Is there really no life more full and no love more amazing than yours? And is it really true that every human should put their faith in such a small and pitiful love?

You would be so much happier and there would be so much more of you if some higher God could smash your tiny, little universe with a hammer, scattering the stars like glitter, and leave you out in the open, just as free as any man to look up to God, as well as down!

It is worthy to note here that the most purely practical sciences do take this view of evil diseases of the mind. Science doesn't try to argue with the disease as if it were a heresy, but instead tries to simply break it like a spell. Neither modern science nor ancient religion believes in completely free thought. Theology discourages certain thoughts by calling them blasphemous. Science discourages certain thoughts by calling them morbid. For example, some religious communities essentially discouraged people from thinking about sex. And the new scientific community definitely discourages people from thinking about death–it is a fact, but it is considered too dark of a fact.

In dealing with those people whose dark minds have a touch of disorder in them, modern science doesn't use pure logic to heal them. In these cases, it is not enough that the unhappy person desires truth; they must desire *health*. Nothing can save them from insanity but an unquenchable thirst for normality, like a tired dog thirsts for water. A person can't think herself out of mental evil, because it is this organ of thought that has become diseased, uncontrollable, and independent. She can only be saved by force of will or by faith. The moment her brain tries to think logically, it moves in the small, circular rut. She will go round and round her logical circle, just as a passenger on London's subway will go round and round the Inner Circle, unless they perform the voluntary, powerful, and mystical act of getting off at Gower Street.

The bottom line here for the madman is to decide. A door must be shut forever. Every remedy at this point is a desperate remedy. Every cure is a miraculous cure. Curing a madman doesn't mean arguing with a philosopher; it means casting out a demon.

The methods of our doctors and psychologists are like those of Bloody Mary, the queen of decapitation. Their attitude is that if the person is to keep on living, they must stop thinking. Their advice is to intellectually amputate. If thy *head* offend thee, cut it off–for it is better not only to enter the Kingdom of Heaven as a child, but to enter Heaven as a dimwit, rather than with your whole brain be cast into Hell– or into Hanwell.

Mad Scientists

This has been my experience with the madman: he usually argues, and many times argues successfully. I am sure he could be beaten using reason, and we could build a logical case against him, but this could be put much more precisely using illustrations. The madman is in the clean and well-lit prison of one idea. Or, to put it differently, he is sharpened to one painful point. There is no healthy doubt or complexity in his brain.

Now, as I explained in the introduction, I have decided in these early chapters not to draw a diagram of a detailed doctrine so much as to paint pictures of a point of view. And I have spent all this time describing my view of the madman for this reason: the madman has the same effect on me as most modern thinkers.

There is an unmistakable atmosphere surrounding Hanwell, and I feel that same atmosphere from half of the leading professors and seats of learning today; most of the mad scientists are mad in more ways than one. They all have exactly what we have noted already–a broad, impressive capacity to think combined with almost no common sense. They are great thinkers only in the sense that they think of one small explanation for things and stretch it out a long way. But a pattern of shapes can stretch forever and still be a small pattern. They see a chess board as white squares on a black surface, and if the whole world were paved with it, they would still see white on black. Like the lunatic, they can't change their perspective. They can't make a mental effort and suddenly see black on white.

The Man Who Believes Everything Began in Matter

First, let's take the more obvious case of materialism–the idea that nothing exists except physical matter. As an explanation of the world, materialism is almost insanely simple. It feels very similar to how a madman would think. In one sense it seemingly explains everything. And, in another sense, it leaves everything out.

Even the arguments of capable and sincere materialists leave us feeling this unique sensation: they understand everything, but everything doesn't seem to be worth understanding. Their universe may be complete down to every bolt and screw, but it is still smaller than our world. Somehow this theory, like the clear, simple theory of the madman, doesn't explain the real things of the earth: fighting tribes, proud mothers, first love, fear on the sea. The earth is so very large, but the universe is so very small. The universe is about the smallest hole that a man can hide his head in.

I hope you understand I am not discussing whether these philosophies are true. Right now, I am only discussing whether they are *healthy*. I hope to later tackle the question of objective truth, but here I am only focused on the effect these philosophies have on the brain. I am not trying at the moment to prove to a materialist that materialism isn't true, just as I didn't prove to the man who thought he was Christ that he was serving for no reason. I only want to point out the fact that both cases have the same kind of completeness and the same kind of incompleteness.

You can explain why a man was sent to Hanwell by saying it was the crucifixion of a god too glorious for this world. That is a good enough explanation. Likewise, you can explain the nature of the universe with materialism, believing that all things, even the souls of men, are just leaves growing inevitably on an unconscious tree—the blind destiny of matter. This is a good explanation, too. It is not, however, quite as good as the madman's.

The point here, however, is that normal people not only push back against both of these explanations, but they push back for the same reason. People generally feel that if the man in the insane asylum is the real God, then he isn't much of a god. And, similarly, if the universe of the materialist is the real universe, then it isn't much of a universe. The thing has shrunk. The god is less godly than many men. And (according to materialists) the whole picture of life is something much more slim, boring, and unimportant than many individual aspects of it. The parts somehow seem greater than the whole.

It is important to note here that the materialist philosophy, as you can see, is much more narrow-minded than any religion. In one sense, of course, all intelligent ideas are narrow. They can't be wider than themselves. A Christian is narrow-minded in the same way that an atheist is narrow-minded; he can't think Christianity is false and continue to be a Christian. And the atheist can't think atheism is false and continue to be an atheist. Everyone has their restrictions on what they can think. But as it turns out, there is a very special way in which materialism is more narrow-minded than spiritualism.

Materialists think I am a slave because I am not allowed to believe in determinism. I think materialists are slaves because they are not allowed to believe in fairies. But if we look at the two restrictions, the materialist's restriction is much more restricting than mine. The Christian is actually quite free to believe in a considerable amount of order and structure in the universe. But the materialist isn't allowed to include into his nice, orderly universe even the slightest hint of a spirit or a miracle, not even the tiniest little elf hiding in a dandelion.

The Christian admits the universe has many miscellaneous parts, just as a sane man knows he is complex. The sane man knows he is made with a touch of the beast, a touch of the devil, a touch of the saint, a touch of the citizen. And the really sane man knows he has a touch of the madman. But the materialist's world is very simple and clear, just as the madman knows clearly that he is sane. The materialist is positive that all of history is simply cause and effect, just as the interesting person mentioned before is quite sure he is a chicken. Materialists and madmen never have doubts.

Spiritual beliefs don't put limits on the mind as materialism does. Even if I believe in immortality, I don't need to think about it. But if I *don't* believe in immortality, then I *must* not think about it. In the first case, the road is clear and I can go as far as I want; in the second case, the road is closed. But the case against materialism gets even stronger, and its connection to madness gets stranger.

Whether right or wrong, our earlier argument against the complete and logical theories of the madman is that it slowly destroyed his humanity. Now, whether right or wrong, our main argument against a man believing only in physical matter is that it gradually destroys his humanity, too. And I don't mean it only destroys his kindness. It destroys hope, courage, poetry, motivation—all that is human. This materialism generally leads to total fatalism—to believing the future is inevitable. And when this process happens, it is quite useless to pretend that it is freeing in any way. It is ridiculous to say you are encouraging freedom when you use your free thought only to destroy a person's free will.

The determinists are here to bind us, not to free us. It is fitting that they call their idea the "chain" of cause and effect. It is the worst chain that ever bound a human being. Materialists can use words like "freedom" and "liberty" if they want, but obviously it is just as irrelevant to use these words here as to use them when speaking of a madman locked up in a madhouse. You can say, if you want, that a person is free to think she is a hard-boiled egg. But surely it is a bigger and more important fact that if she is a hard-boiled egg, then she isn't free to eat, drink, sleep, walk, or smoke a cigarette. Likewise, you can say if you want that the determinist is free not to believe in the reality of free will. But it is a bigger and more important fact that she isn't free to raise a hand, to curse, to thank, to justify, to urge, to punish, to resist temptations, to rally mobs, to make New Year's resolutions, to pardon sinners, to resist tyrants, or even to say "thank you" for the mustard.

The Man Who Believes Everything Began in Himself

The materialist, of course, is not the only one of which this is true. It also applies to the man on the opposite end of the philosophical spectrum. There is a skeptic who is more dangerous than the man who believes everything began in physical matter. It is possible you may meet the man who believes everything began in himself. He doesn't doubt the existence of angels or demons, but he does doubt the existence of men and cows. According to him, his own friends are imaginary, a myth he made up. Out of his head he created his own father and mother.

This horrible thought attracts people because of the sort of mystical self-centeredness of our day. That publisher who thought men would be alright if they believed in themselves, those seekers of the superior man, who are always looking for him in the mirror, those writers who talk about finding themselves, all these people are inches away from this awful emptiness.

Now, when this friendly world all around the man has been erased like a lie, when friends disappear like ghosts, and the foundations of the world crumble, then, when the man who believes in nothing but himself is alone in his own nightmare, his great individualistic motto will be ironically and vengefully written over him. The stars will be only dots in the blackness of his own brain. His mother's face will be only a sketch drawn by his own insane pencil on the walls of his cell. But there, over his cell, will be written these tragically true words: "He believes in himself."

All that matters here, however, is to note how this extreme hyper-selfishness displays the same paradox as materialism. It is equally complete as an argument and equally crippling when applied to the real world. To make things simple, it is easier to explain the idea by saying a man can believe he is always in a dream. Now, obviously there isn't any way to prove to him that he isn't dreaming, because we can't say anything to him that couldn't also be said in a dream. But if the man began to burn down London while claiming his wife would soon wake him up for breakfast, then we should take him and put him with the other logical thinkers in a place we have talked about often throughout this chapter.

The man who can't believe his senses and the man who can't believe anything but his senses are both insane, but their insanity isn't proven by any flaw in their argument. It is proven by the enormous mess of their whole lives. They have both locked themselves in separate boxes, painted on the inside with the sun and the stars. They are both unable to get out—the materialist into the health and happiness of Heaven, and the self-believer into even the health and happiness of

Earth. Their position makes enough sense; in a way, it is infinitely logical, just as a penny is infinitely circular. But there is such a thing as a bad infinity, an eternity of slavery.

It is funny to notice how many modern thinkers, whether skeptics or mystics, have adopted a certain eastern symbol as their sign, which represents perfectly this eternal meaninglessness. When they want to represent eternity, they choose the symbol of a snake with his tail in his mouth. I find the image of that very disappointing meal to be shockingly sarcastic. The eternity of the materialists, the eternity of the eastern pessimists, the eternity of the arrogant higher scientists of today is, indeed, very well represented by a snake eating his tail–a disgraced animal who destroys even himself.

What Keeps a Man Sane?

This chapter is purely practical and focuses on the main mark of insanity. We can say, in summary, that it is reason without a foundation, reason in the void. The man who begins to think without the right foundation goes insane. He begins his thinking at the wrong starting point. And for the rest of this book, we must try and discover the right starting point. If some things drive men crazy, what is it that keeps them sane? By the end of this book, I hope to give a well-defined (some will think a far too well-defined) answer.

For the moment, however, it is possible, in a simple way, to give a general answer about what has kept men sane throughout real human history. Mysticism keeps men sane. As long as you have mystery, you have health. When you destroy mystery, you create a dark disease.

The ordinary man has always been sane because the ordinary man has always been a mystic. He allows the twilight. He has always had one foot in earth and the other in fairyland. He has always left himself free to doubt his gods. But (unlike the agnostics of today) free also to believe in them. He has always cared more for truth than for consistency. If he saw two truths that seemed to contradict each other, he would accept the two truths and the contradiction along with them. He sees spiritually from two different points, just like his physical sight. He sees two different pictures at once, but he sees better because of it. What I mean is that he has always believed there was such a thing as fate, but also such a thing as free will. He believed that children would inherit the Kingdom of Heaven, but nevertheless should be obedient to the kingdom of earth. He admired youth because it was young and admired age because it wasn't. It is this balance of what seems like contradictions that has kept the healthy man afloat.

The whole secret of mysticism is this: a person can understand everything only with the help of what they don't understand. The dark, diseased thinker tries to make everything understandable, and succeeds in making everything mysterious. The mystic allows one thing to be mysterious, and everything else is understood. The determinist makes the theory of cause and effect quite clear, and then finds that he can't say "water, please" to a waitress. The Christian allows free will to remain a holy mystery, but because of this, her interactions with the waitress become sparklingly clear. She plants the seed of blind belief in a central, dark place, but it grows out from there in all directions with an abundance of naturally healthy branches.

We have already taken the circle as the symbol of both logic and madness, so we may as well take the cross as the symbol of both mystery and health. Buddhism is centripetal, meaning everything falls to the center. Christianity is centrifugal, meaning everything pushes away from the center and breaks out. The circle is perfect and infinite in its nature, but it can never change its size; it can never be larger or smaller. But the cross, even though it has a collision and a contradiction at its heart, can extend its four arms forever without transforming its shape. Because it has a paradox at its center, it can grow without changing. The circle is bound to go round and round forever, but the cross opens its arms to the four winds; it is a signpost for free travelers.

The Mother of Lunatics

Even symbols like the cross or circle are sometimes imperfect when speaking of this deep topic, but another symbol from nature will explain well enough the real effects of mysticism on mankind. The one thing in God's creation that we can't look at is the one thing that lights up everything we see. Like the sun at noon time, mysticism explains everything else by the light of its own victorious invisibility. Logic without a foundation is (in the exact sense of a popular phrase) all moonshine. It is nonsense. It is light without heat, and it is secondary light reflected from a dead world. But the Greeks were on to something when they made Apollo the god of both imagination and sanity; he had power over poetry *and* healing.

That mysticism by which all men live plays the same role as the sun in the sky. We are aware of it as a kind of wonderful confusion; it is something both shining and shapeless, both a blaze and a blur. But the circular shape of the moon is as clear and unmistakable, as repeated and redundant, as a perfect circle in a geometry book. Because like geometry, the moon is utterly reasonable; the moon is the mother of lunatics, and she has given them all her name.

3

The Suicide of Thought

Common phrases and sayings can not only be powerful, but also precise. A figure of speech can often get into a crack too small for a definition. A phrase like "off color" might have been coined by some famous novelist as she tried, in agony, to express exactly what she meant. And there isn't a popular phrase more precise than this: "His heart is in the right place."

This phrase involves the idea of normal proportions. Not only do hearts exist, but they should also be in right relation to other organs. A heart in the *wrong* place would accurately describe the kind of deranged forgiveness and twisted kindness of the average modern thinker. They may have a heroically large and generous heart, but it may not be in the right place. Likewise, most modern societies and cultures lack this sense of normal proportions.

Virtues Gone Wild

The modern world is not evil. In some ways, the modern world is far too good. It is full of wild and wasted goodness.

When a religion is shattered (as Christianity was shattered at the Reformation), the vices of the religion are not the only thing unleashed into the world. The vices are, to be sure, unleashed, and they wander and destroy things. But the virtues are unleashed, too. These virtues wander more wildly than the vices, and they cause more terrible destruction.

The modern world is full of the old Christian virtues gone wild. They have been cut off from each other, and they wander alone. For example, some people care for the virtue of truth, but their truth has no kindness toward others. Likewise, some only care about kindness, but their kindness (I'm sorry to say) is often untruthful. But we can find a much stronger example of misplaced virtue in the case of man's misplacement of humility.

The main purpose of humility is to restrain man's arrogance and never-ending desire, because our own newly invented needs always seem to outpace our blessings. Our ability to enjoy destroys half our joys. By asking for pleasure, we lose the best pleasure of all, which is surprise. It becomes clear that if a person wants to make their world large, then they should always be making themselves small. The loftiest dreams, the tallest cities, and the highest pinnacles were all created by humility. Giants that stomp down forests like grass are the creations of humility. Towers that reach up to the loneliest star are creations of humility. Because towers are not tall unless we look up at them, and giants are not giant unless they are larger than us. All this gigantic imagination, which might be the greatest of man's pleasures, is completely humble at its core. It is impossible to enjoy anything without humility–even pride.

What we suffer from today, however, is humility in the wrong place. Humility has moved from the place of inward ambition to the place of outward conviction, where it was never meant to be. We were meant to have doubts about ourselves, but never to have doubts about the truth. This has been completely reversed. Nowadays the thing in which a person does believe in is exactly the thing he shouldn't–himself. And the thing he doubts is exactly the thing he shouldn't doubt–his God-given ability to think. The new kind of skeptic is so humble that he doubts if he can learn anything at all.

It would have been wrong, then, if we had said without thinking that there is no humility in today's age. The truth is that there is a real humility very common in today's age, but this humility is poisonous. Healthy humility is like a prod that keeps you from stopping, not a nail in your shoe that keeps you from going on. Healthy humility makes a man doubt himself and his own efforts, which might make him work harder. But the new humility makes a man doubt his work, which will make him stop working altogether.

If you listen to any common discussion, you will likely hear someone say that he "may be wrong," or that his view "might not be right." But of course he thinks his view is the right one, or it wouldn't be his view. We are on the road to producing a society too mentally humble to believe in the multiplication table. We are in danger of having scientists who doubt the law of gravity, considering it simply a nice little thought of their own. Skeptics used to be too proud and too set in their ideas to be convinced, but modern skeptics are too *humble* to be convinced. The meek really do inherit the earth, but the modern skeptics are too meek to even claim their inheritance. It is this intellectual helplessness that is our second problem.

The Authority to Think

The last chapter focused on one fact of observation: the danger of mental disease lies in logic, not in imagination. The chapter didn't mean to attack the authority of logic. Its purpose was actually to defend it, because it needs defending. The whole modern world is at war with reason, and its walls already shake.

It is commonly said that our strongest thinkers can't see any answer to the riddle of religion–they don't know why it exists. But the trouble with our thinkers is not that they can't see the answer, it is that they can't even see the riddle. For instance, the modern free thinkers speak of religious authority not only as if there were no reason in it, but as if there had never been any reason *for* it. Apart from appreciating the philosophical side of it, they can't see why it ever came around in the first place.

Religious authority has often, without a doubt, abused its power and been cruel or unreasonable, just as every legal system (especially our current one) has been hard and cold-hearted. It is reasonable to criticize the police, just as it's reasonable to criticize religious authority. Some might even say it's glorious. But those who attack religious authority without knowing why it exists are like men who attack the police without ever having heard of burglars.

The human mind is in great potential danger–a danger as real as burglary. Against this danger, religious authority (whether right or wrong) was raised by humanity to be a barrier. Some barrier, at least, needs to be raised against this danger, if humanity intends to avoid total ruin. The danger I am speaking of is that the human brain is free to destroy itself. One generation of humans can prevent the very existence of the next generation, either by drowning themselves in the ocean or by all taking a vow of chastity. Similarly, one generation of thinkers can, to some degree, prevent future thinking by teaching the next generation that there is no validity in human thought.

It is pointless to talk about reason and faith as opposites. Reason itself is a matter of faith. It is an act of faith to claim our thoughts have any relation to reality at all. If you are a true skeptic, if you truly question everything, then you must sooner or later ask yourself the question, "Why should *any* of our thinking be sound, even our most basic observations and conclusions? Why shouldn't good logic be as misleading as bad logic? They are both just movements in the brain of a bewildered ape." The young skeptic says, "I have a right to think for myself." But the old, true skeptic says, "I have no right to think for myself. I have no right to think at all."

There happens to be one thought a person can have that stops all other thought, and that thought is the only thought that should be stopped. That thought is the ultimate evil that all religious authority defends against. It only appears at the end of morally bankrupt times like our own, and already H.G. Wells has raised its ruinous banner. He has written a piece in which he questions the brain itself, claiming his thoughts have no relation to reality at all.

It is this destruction of the brain that all the organized efforts of religion were originally formed against. The creeds and the crusades, the church hierarchies and horrible persecutions were not organized to suppress reason, as some may say. They were organized for the difficult *defense* of reason. Somehow man knew that if things began to be questioned, the brain would be questioned first. The authority of priests to forgive, the authority of popes to define the authority, even the authority of inquisitors to terrify, these were all only dark walls built around the one central authority they didn't want to be touched, the authority more supernatural and more disprovable than all: the authority of a man to think.

We know now that this is true. We don't have an excuse for *not* knowing it. Even now we can hear skepticism crashing through those old walls of authorities, and at the same time we can see reason shaking on her throne. Just as religion is gone today, reason is gone tomorrow. Because both religion and reason are foundational and authoritative. They are both used to prove things, but neither of them can be proven themselves. And while we have been undermining religious authority, we have also to a great extent undermined that human authority that allows us to solve two plus two. With a long, hard tug we have tried to pull the hat off the Pope, and his head has come off with it.

Thoughts That Stop Thought

Some may say I haven't sufficiently supported my argument. So, even though it may be dull, we should run through the main modern trends of thought that manage to stop thought itself.

Evolution

The two philosophies presented in the last chapter–the idea that nothing is real beyond the material and the idea that nothing is real beyond yourself–have this thought-stopping effect. If the mind is simply a machine, then thought can't be very exciting, and if the universe isn't real, then there is nothing to think about. But in these cases, the effect is indirect and debatable. In some cases, however, the effect is direct and clear, most notably in the case of what we generally call evolution.

Evolution is a good example of that modern idea that, if it destroys anything, it destroys itself. Evolution is either an innocent scientific explanation for how certain things on earth came to be, or, if it is anything more than this, it is an attack on thought itself. Evolution doesn't destroy religion. If it destroys anything, it destroys rationalism.

If evolution simply means that something called an ape turned very slowly into something called a human, then it is harmless to even the most orthodox; a personal God might just as well do things slowly as do things quickly, especially if he were outside time, like the Christian God. But if it means anything more, then it means there is no such thing as an ape to change from, and no such thing as a man for him to change into. It means that there is no such thing as a *thing*. At best, there is only one thing, and that thing is a constant flow of anything and everything. This isn't an attack on faith, it is an attack on the *mind*. You can't think if there aren't any things to think about. You can't think if you aren't separate from the concept of thought. Descartes said, "I think; therefore, I am." The philosophical evolutionist reverses it and makes it a negative. He says, "I am not; therefore, I cannot think."

Then there is the opposite attack on thought–the insistence that every separate thing is "unique," and there are no categories for anything at all. This also is simply destructive. Thinking means connecting things, and thinking stops when they can't be connected. It should be obvious that this skepticism forbidding thought must also stop speech, too; we couldn't open our mouths without contradicting them. When H.G. Wells said, "All chairs are quite different," he wasn't only wrong, but he also contradicted himself. If all chairs are quite different, we couldn't categorize them as "all chairs."

The False Theory of Progress

A similar modern trend is the false theory of "progress," which suggests we should change the test instead of trying to pass the test. We have heard it said many times that "what is right in one time is wrong in another." This is logical enough if it means there is a fixed goal in mind, and that certain methods reach that goal at certain times and not at other times. Let's say that if one general goal of women is to be elegant, then it might be an improvement to grow thicker at one time in history and to grow thinner at another. But you can't say women are improving by no longer wishing to be elegant and beginning to wish to be oblong. If the standard changes, how can there be improvement? Improvement implies a standard you are improving toward.

Friedrich Nietzsche started a nonsensical idea that what people now call "good" is what people used to call "evil." If that were true, we couldn't say we are doing better (or even worse) than them. How can you pull ahead of someone if you are walking in the other direction? It is impossible to debate whether one culture was more successful in being happy than another culture was successful in being miserable. It would be like discussing whether Milton was more virtuous than a pig is fat.

It is true that a person (a ridiculous person) might make change itself their ideal–that the goal simply is for things to continually change. But as a goal, change itself becomes unchangeable. If the change-worshipper wants to measure their own progress toward change, they must be seriously committed to the goal of change. They can't begin to flirt with the goal of sameness. Progress itself can't progress. The main point, however, is that this idea of a fundamental change in goals is one of those things that make thought about the past or future simply impossible. The idea of completely altering the goal or standard in the middle of human history doesn't just take from us the pleasure of honoring our ancestors–it even takes the more modern and sophisticated pleasure of despising them.

Extreme Pragmatism

This simple summary of the thought-destroying forces of our time wouldn't be complete without somehow connecting it to pragmatism–the idea of judging ideas or beliefs by their practical use in the real world. I have been pragmatic already in this book, and I hope to always use pragmatism to find the truth. But there is an extreme way it could be used that involves the absence of any and all truth. Let me quickly explain.

I agree with the pragmatists that objective truth–the truth regardless of personal feelings, perspectives, opinions, etc.–isn't all that matters, and that we humans have a foundational need to believe whatever is necessary for our minds to function. But I think that one of those necessary things *is a belief in objective truth*. The pragmatist tells a man to think what he needs to think in order to get on with his life and to disregard the objective or Absolute. But one of the things he really needs to think about *happens to be the Absolute*.

This philosophy really is a kind of puzzle. Pragmatism is concerned with human needs, and one of the primary human needs is to be something more than a pragmatist. Extreme pragmatism is just as inhuman as the determinism it attacks so strongly. The determinist (who, to be fair, doesn't pretend to be a human being) sees nonsense in the human perception of choice. The pragmatist, who claims to be especially human, sees nonsense in the human perception of an objective fact.

No More Questions Left to Ask

To summarize our argument so far, we may say that the most popular current philosophies have not only a hint of madness, but also a hint of *suicidal* madness—a madness that destroys itself. The common questioner has beaten his head against the limits of human thought, and he has cracked it. It is pointless now for the orthodox and the great thinkers to warn against the dangerous, childish ways of free thought. Because this isn't the childhood of free thought; it is the old age and ultimate *conclusion* of free thought. It is pointless to discuss what terrible things will happen if wild skepticism runs its course, because it *has* run its course. It is pointless for eloquent atheists to speak about the great truths that will be revealed if we ever see free thought begin, because we have seen it *end*. It has no more questions to ask; it has even questioned itself. You can't think of any crazier dream than a city in which people ask themselves if they have a self. You couldn't ask for a more skeptical world than one in which people doubt if there is a world.

I am sure we could have reached the bottom of the doubting barrel more quickly and cleanly if we hadn't been held back weakly by the indefensible claim that it is blasphemy or the ridiculous notion that modern England is a Christian nation. But it would have reached the bottom anyway. Outspoken atheists are still unfairly persecuted, but it is because they are an old minority rather than new. Free thought has used up its own freedom. It is worn out from its own success. If any enthusiastic free thinker still cheers on philosophic freedom as the dawn of a new day, he has come outside to see the sun rise only just in time to see it set.

We have no more questions left to ask. We have looked for questions in the darkest corners and on the wildest mountains. We have found all the questions that can be found. It is about time we give up looking for questions and begin looking for answers.

Embracing a World of Limits

I have one more thing to add. At the beginning of this book, I said our mental ruin has been caused by wild logic, not by wild imagination. A man doesn't go insane by making a statue a mile high, but he might go insane if he measured it out in square inches. Now, one school of thought has jumped on this idea and has tried to use it as a way to bring back a pagan health to the world. They admit that reason destroys, but they say Will, the mental faculty that allows a person to decide and act on a decision, creates. The ultimate authority, they say, is in the will, not in reason. The primary point is not why a man demands a thing, but simply the fact that he does demand it.

I don't have time to trace back or explain this philosophy of Will. I suppose it came through Nietzsche, who preached something called egoism, that selfishness is the motivation for all decisions. That turned out to be simple-minded enough, because Nietzsche undermined egoism just by preaching it. To preach anything is to give that thing to others. First, the egoist calls life a war with no mercy, and then he goes to the greatest possible trouble to train his enemies in war. To preach selfishness is to practice selflessness.

However it began, the view is common enough in current discourse. The main defense of these thinkers is that they say they aren't thinkers–they are *makers*. They say that choice itself is the highest thing. In this way, Bernard Shaw attacks the old idea that men's actions are to be judged by how happy they make him. He says that a man doesn't do things for his own happiness, but instead decides to do things just for the sake of deciding. He doesn't say, "Butter will make me happy," but instead, "I want butter." Even H.G. Wells speaks as if he is half-convinced. He says we should measure the quality of our actions not as a thinker would, but like an artist, saying, "I *feel* that color is right," or, "that line *will* go there." They are all excited, because with this theory of the great authority of Will, they think they can break out of the hopeless prison of rationalism. They think they can escape. But they can't. This worship of will ends in the same destruction and emptiness as the pursuit of pure logic. Just as completely free thought involves the doubting of thought itself, the general pursuit of "willing" actually paralyzes the will.

These people don't see the real difference between the old useful test of happiness (though it is awkward, of course, and easily misunderstood) and the test they suggest. The real difference between the test of happiness and the test of will is simple: the test of happiness is a test, and the other isn't. You can debate whether a man's act of jumping over a cliff was for the sake of happiness. You can't debate whether it came from will. *Of course* it did. You can applaud an action because it brought pleasure or pain, for discovering truth or saving the soul, but you can't praise an action because it simply shows will. If you say that, all you are really saying is that someone simply made a decision. With this worship of will, you can't really choose one course of action as better than any other. And yet choosing one course as better than another is exactly what we mean by "making a decision." It's literally the definition of the will you are worshipping.

The worship of will is the denial of will. To admire the idea of choice means to refuse to choose. If a will-worshipper comes to me and says, "Choose something," that's the same as saying, "I don't care what you choose," and that's the same as saying, "I have no choice in the matter." Nietzsche and the rest of the will-worshippers don't really have the power to decide. They can't will. They can hardly wish.

If anyone wants proof of this, I can give it to them quite easily. The proof can be found in this fact, that they always talk of will as something that expands and breaks out. But it is really the opposite. With every choice you make, you limit yourself. To desire action is to desire limitation. In that sense, every act is an act of self-sacrifice. When you choose anything, you reject everything else. This can be used to describe marriage, but it can also be used to explain every other act. With every act you choose to do, you irreversibly select one action and exclude all others. Just as when you marry one woman, you give up all the other women, so it goes that when you take one course of action, you give up all the other courses. If you become the King of England, you have to quit your job as cashier at the grocery store. If you move to Rome, you sacrifice a glamorous life in Wimbledon.

It is the existence of this limiting aspect of will that makes most of what the anarchic will-worshipper says only slightly better than gibberish. For example, they tell us to never say "thou shalt not." But surely it is obvious that "thou shalt not" is naturally connected to "I will." "I will go to the theater, and thou shalt not stop me."

Anarchism urges us to be bold creative artists and to care for no laws or limits. But art *is* limitation; the essential feature of every painting is the frame. If you draw a giraffe, you must draw him with a long neck. If, in your bold creativity, you think you are free to draw a giraffe with a short neck, you will find that you really aren't free to draw a giraffe at all. The moment you step into a world of facts, you step into a world of limits. You can free something from foreign laws, but not from the laws that define its nature.

If you wanted, you could free a tiger from his cage. But please don't free him from his stripes. Don't free a camel from the burden of his hump. In that case, you might be freeing him from being a camel. Don't go around as a rabble-rouser, encouraging triangles to break out of the prison of their three sides. If a triangle breaks out of its three sides, its life comes to a sorrowful end. Somebody wrote a work called "The Loves of the Triangles." I never read it, but I am sure that if triangles were ever loved, they were loved for being triangular. This certainly is the case with all artistic creation, which is in some ways the clearest and most conclusive example of pure will. The artist loves his limitations. They help form the thing he is doing. The painter is glad the canvas is flat. The sculptor is glad the clay is colorless.

In case the point isn't clear, an example from history may illustrate it–the French Revolution. The most influential anti-Royalty political group, the Jacobins, wanted to have something specific and limited. They desired the freedoms of democracy, but also the vetoes of democracy. They wished to have votes and not to have kings. Therefore, they created something with a solid body and shape: the clearly defined square of social equality and wealth for the poverty-stricken people of France. But since then, this revolutionary, risk-taking mind of Europe has been weakened by a rejection of limits. Liberalism, a philosophy based on liberty and equality, has been degraded into liberality, to being open to any and all philosophies.

The Jacobin could tell you not only the system he would rebel against, but more importantly, he could tell you the system he would not rebel against, the system he would trust. But the new rebel is a skeptic and won't entirely trust anything. He has no loyalty; therefore, he can never really be a revolutionist. And the fact that he doubts everything trips him up when he wants to reject anything. Because all rejection implies a moral doctrine of some kind, and the modern revolutionist doubts not only the institution he rejects, but the moral doctrine which allows him to reject it.

So, as a politician, he will cry out that war is a waste of human life, and then, as a philosopher, that all life is a waste of time. As a Russian pessimist, he will criticize a policeman for killing a peasant, and then use the highest philosophies to

45

prove that the peasant should have killed himself. He will denounce marriage as a lie, then he will denounce rich degenerates for treating it as a lie. The man of this philosophy first goes to a political meeting where he complains that primitive people are treated as if they were beasts. Then, he takes his hat and umbrella and goes to a scientific meeting where he proves that they practically are beasts.

In short, the modern revolutionist, being an infinite skeptic, is always trying to undermine his own mines. In his book on politics, he attacks men for stomping on morality; in his book on ethics, he attacks morality for stomping on men. Because of this, the modern rebel has become practically useless for anything having to do with rebellion. By rebelling against everything, he has lost his right to rebel against anything.

The Disappearance of Satire

I may add here that we can see the same destructive emptiness in certain types of literature, especially in satire. Satire may be insane and chaotic, but it admits there is superiority in certain things over others; it assumes some kind of standard. When little boys in the street laugh at the fatness of some famous writer (you are reading his book) they are unconsciously assuming a standard of Greek gods. They are comparing him to the marble statue of Apollo. And the strange disappearance of satire today is an example of the aggressive things going away because there aren't any principles to be aggressive about.

> ## ◎   A Weighty Matter   ◎
>
> Let's not sugar-coat it – Chesterton was fat. His size was so considerable that, upon his passing, his casket could not be carried down the stairs of his house and instead was sent out a second-story window. P.G. Wodehouse captured the essence of his figure when he humorously likened the sound of a loud crash to "G.K. Chesterton falling onto a sheet of tin." In another jest, the rail-thin George Bernard Shaw once remarked to Chesterton, "If I were as fat as you, I'd hang myself." Chesterton, displaying his wit, replied, "If I were to hang myself, I would use you for the rope." While his approach to personal health might invite discussion, it's worth noting that Chesterton shares the company of other celebrated Christians on the heavier side, including Thomas Aquinas and St. John XXIII.

Nietzsche had some natural talent for sarcasm. He could smirk, but he couldn't laugh. But there has never been any real weight to his satire because it simply doesn't have any mass of common moral standard behind it. Nietzsche himself is more absurd than anything he mocks. But, if nothing else, Nietzsche makes a very good example of the average victim of a mental breakdown. The dementia and the softening of the brain which overtook him in the end was not a physical attack. If Nietzsche hadn't ended in stupidity, then at least Nietzscheism would end in stupidity. Thinking in isolation and with pride always ends in being an idiot. Everyone who will not let their heart be softened will at least have softening of the brain.

This last attempt to dodge intellectualism has ended in intellectualism—and because of that, in death. The mission has failed. The wild worship of lawlessness and the materialist worship of law both end in the same emptiness. Nietzsche scales staggering heights, but he turns up ultimately in the Buddhist mountains of Tibet. He sits down beside Tolstoy in the land of nothing and Nirvana.

Tolstoy is frozen in decision by a Buddhist instinct that all special actions are evil. But Nietzsche is equally frozen by his view that all special actions are good. Because if all special actions are good, then none of them are special. They are both helpless, standing at the crossroads–Tolstoy hates all the roads and Nietzsche likes all the roads. The result is–well, some things are not hard to calculate. They continue to stand at the crossroads.

A Surprising Sanity

Here I will end (thank God) the first and most boring business of this book–the basic, raw review of recent thought. After this I will begin to paint a picture of life that may not interest the reader, but at least it interests me. In front of me, as I finish this chapter, is a pile of modern books I have been pouring through for the sake of this project. It is both a pile of innovation and a pile of uselessness.

Due to the happy accident of my current project, I can see the inevitable philosophical collision of Arthur Schopenhauer and Tolstoy, Nietzsche and Bernard Shaw, as clearly as an inevitable train wreck could be seen from a hot air balloon. They are all on the road to the emptiness of the insane asylum. For insanity could be defined as using mental energy for the sake of reaching mental helplessness, and they have almost reached it. Whoever thinks he is made of glass is working toward the destruction of thought, because glass can't think. So, he who decides to reject nothing is really deciding to destroy his ability to decide, because will is not only the choice of something, but also the rejection of almost everything. And as I flip through page after page of clever, wonderful, tiresome, and useless modern books, one of them catches my eye. It is called *Jeanne d'Arc* by Anatole France. I have only glanced at it, but a glance was enough to remind me of Ernest Renan's *Vie de Jesus*. It follows the same strange method of the devoted skeptic.

I don't mention either book just to criticize it, but because their titles reminded me of two surprising examples of Sanity that blew all the books in front of me out of the water. Joan of Arc wasn't stuck at the crossroads, either by rejecting all paths like Tolstoy or by accepting them all like Nietzsche. She chose a path and went down it like a lightning bolt. And yet I realized, when I really thought about her, that Joan contained in her all that was true in either Tolstoy or Nietzsche, all that was even tolerable in either of them.

I thought of everything admirable in Tolstoy: the pleasure in little things, especially in simple compassion, the appreciation for the earth, the admiration for the poor, the dignity of the bowed back. Joan of Arc had all that and more. She not only admired poverty, but she *lived* it, whereas Tolstoy is a typical rich man trying to find out its secret. And then I thought of everything brave and proud and pitiable in poor Nietzsche, and his rebellion against the emptiness and cowardice of our time. I thought of his cry for the blissful balance of battle, his hunger for the rush of great war horses, his thirst to fight. Well, Joan of Arc had all that and more, too. She didn't praise fighting, she *fought*. We know that she wasn't afraid of an army, while Nietzsche, for all we know, was afraid of a cow.

Tolstoy only praised the peasant; she *was* the peasant. Nietzsche only praised the warrior; she *was* the warrior. She beat them both at their own opposite goals. She was more gentle than Tolstoy and more violent than Nietzsche. And yet she was a perfectly practical person who actually did something, while they were just wild philosophers who did nothing. I couldn't help but think that she and her faith may have had a secret of moral unity and usefulness that we have lost. And with that thought came a larger one, and the gigantic figure of her Master crossed my mind.

The same modern tendency which troubled the work of Anatole France also troubled that of Ernest Renan. Renan also separated Christ's love from his anger. Renan even explained his righteous anger at the Temple as simply a nervous breakdown caused by his expectations to be perfect. Renan thinks it is impossible to have both a love for humanity and a hatred for inhumanity. Altruists, with thin and weak voices, denounce Christ for being an egoist. Egoists, with even thinner and weaker voices, denounce Christ for being an altruist. A huge and heroic sanity exists, but some people can only collect bits and pieces of it. There is a giant of whom they can only see the severed arms and legs walking around. They have torn the soul of Christ into ridiculous parts, labeled them "egoism" and "altruism," and then are just as confused by his insane magnificence and his insane meekness. They have torn his garments and split them, casting lots for his clothes; they don't realize his robe was woven from top to bottom without a seam to split.

4

The Ethics of Elfland

The old often criticize the dreamy idealism of the young. They say, "Ah, yes, when people are young, they have these abstract ideals and these great castles in the sky, but when they reach middle age, these dreams break up like clouds. They give in to a life of politics, to using the tools they have and moving on with the world as it really is."

Respected and generous old men used to say things like this to me when I was a boy. But I have grown up, and I have discovered these generous old men were telling lies. What actually happened is exactly the opposite of what they said would happen. They said I would lose my ideals and begin to believe in the methods of party politicians. But I haven't lost my ideals at all. My faith in fundamental truths is exactly what it always was. What I have lost, however, is my old childlike faith in party politics. I am still just as concerned with the Battle of Armageddon, but I am not as concerned about the General Election. As a baby I hopped up on my mother's knee at the mere mention of politics.

These old men have got it wrong. The dream is always solid and reliable. The dream is always a fact. It is the reality that is often a fraud. As much as I ever have–more than I ever have–I believe in the ideal of Liberty. But there was a rosy time of innocence when I believed in Liberals.

The Definition of Democracy

I use Liberty as an example of one of my lasting convictions because, as I now try to trace the history of my thoughts, I think this conviction may be the only one in which I am biased. I was raised to respect individual freedom, and I have always believed in democracy–in the simple doctrine of a self-governing humanity.

If anyone finds this phrase vague or unclear, I can pause for a moment to explain what I mean by "democracy." It can be stated in two propositions. The first is this: the things that are common to all humanity are more important than the things specific to any one individual. Common, ordinary things are more valuable than extraordinary things–no, they are more extraordinary. *Man* is something more awe-inspiring than *men*, something more strange. The fact that a human exists at all should always seem more miraculous than anything they have accomplished–any power, intellect, art, or civilization. The average person on two legs, then, should feel more heartbreaking than any love song and more exaggerated than any caricature. Death by natural causes is more tragic than even death by starvation. Having a nose at all is more comedic than having a crooked nose.

So, the first principle of democracy is that the most important things in humanity are the things we have in common, not the things unique to individuals. And the second principle is simply this: one of these things that we have in common is an instinctual desire to be involved in politics. Democracy's argument is that governing isn't anything like playing the piano, painting on canvas, discovering the North Pole (an insidious habit of ours), building a subway, or flying a spaceship. Because we don't want anyone to do these things at all unless they do them well. On the other hand, governing *is* like a person writing their own love letters or blowing their own nose. We want people to do these things for themselves, even if they do them badly.

I am not here to argue this is true for everyone. I know some modern people are asking scientists to choose their spouses for them, and maybe soon, for all I know, they will be asking nurses to blow their noses. All I am saying is that mankind really does recognize these things that all humans should do, and that democracy puts governing the community right there beside blowing your own nose. To put it simply, democracy believes that the most important things must be done by ordinary people themselves: the mating of men and women, the raising of children, and the creation of laws. This is democracy, and I have always believed in this.

Democracy and Tradition

There is one thing I have never been able to understand, even when I was a kid. I have never been able to understand where people got the idea that democracy is in any way opposed to tradition. It is obvious that tradition itself is simply democracy stretched out across time. Tradition means trusting the consensus of many common voices rather than trusting one isolated or random account. The man who quotes some German historian rather than the tradition of the

Church, for instance, is only trusting in the upper class. He is trusting in the superiority of one expert as opposed to the daunting authority of a mob. It is easy to see why a fable is treated, and should be treated, more respectfully than a history book. The fable is generally made by the majority of the people in the village, who happen to be sane. The book is written by the one person in the village who is insane.

Those who warn against tradition, claiming people in the past were ignorant, may go ahead and warn against it if they want, along with the claim that voters in the ghetto are ignorant. But those claims won't work for us. If we place great importance on the consensus of ordinary people when dealing with normal, daily things, then there shouldn't be any reason to disregard their consensus when dealing with histories or fables.

Tradition could be defined as an extension of the right to vote. Tradition means giving votes to the most obscure of all people groups: our ancestors. It is the democracy of the dead. Tradition refuses to submit to the small and arrogant oligarchy of those who just happen to be alive and walking around. Democracy commands us to count a person's vote regardless of their class; tradition commands us to count a person's vote regardless of their death. Democracy tells us not to neglect a good man's opinion, even if he is our servant; tradition asks us not to neglect a good man's opinion, even if he is our father. I may be the only one, but I can't separate the two ideas of democracy and tradition. It seems evident that they are the same idea. So, the dead should attend our council meetings. The ancient Greeks voted with stones, so the dead shall vote with tombstones. This is all quite orderly and official, because most tombstones, like most ballots, are marked with a cross.

I would like to say first, then, that if I have had a bias, it was always a bias in favor of democracy, and therefore of tradition. Before we begin with more logical or theoretical arguments, I am fine with accepting that personal bias; I have always been more inclined to believe the crowd of hard-working people than to believe that unique and troublesome literary group to which I belong. I even prefer the biases and prejudices of the people who see life from inside of it rather than the clearest presentations of those who stand on the outside looking in. I would always trust the old wives' fables against the old maids' facts.

Now, I must piece together my general attitude on things, and I don't pretend to have any training in this. I think I will do it, then, by writing down one after another the three or four fundamental ideas that I have found for myself, and pretty much in the way I found them. Then I will roughly combine them, summing up my personal philosophy or untaught religion. Then I will describe my unexpected discovery that the whole thing had been discovered before. It had been discovered by Christianity. Of these profound beliefs that I need to reveal in order, the first had to do with this idea of democracy and tradition. And without the previous explanation of democracy and tradition, I don't think I could make my mental journey clear. I'm not sure if I can make it clear at this point, either, but I will give it a go.

Law and Magic: The Fairy Tale Philosophy

My first and last philosophy, the one I believe in with unbroken confidence, I learned in the nursery. I generally learned it from a nanny, from that saintly priestess appointed

by the stars to protect democracy and tradition. The things I
believed in most back then (and the things I believe in most
now) are the things called fairy tales. They seem to me to be
the totally reasonable things. They are not fantasies; compared with them, other things are fantastic. Compared with
them, religion and rationalism are both unusual, although religion is unusually right and rationalism is unusually
wrong. Fairyland is nothing but the sunny country of common sense.

It isn't earth that judges Heaven, but Heaven that judges
earth. So, for me at least, it wasn't earth that judged elfland,
but elfland that judged earth. I knew the magic beanstalk before I had tasted beans; I was certain of the Man in the Moon
before I was certain of the moon. This is consistent with all
of popular tradition. Modern minor poets are naturalists and
they write about the sand and the sea. But the singers of the
old epics and fables were *super*naturalists, and they sang of
the gods of the sand and sea. Old nannies don't tell children
about the grass, but about the fairies that dance on the
grass, and the old Greeks couldn't see the trees for the dryads.

We should focus here, however, on what kind of morals
and philosophies come from being raised on fairy tales. If I
were describing these tales individually, I could note many
noble and healthy lessons they teach. There is the gentle-
manly lesson of *Jack the Giant Killer*–that giants should be
killed because they are gigantic. It is a manly mutiny against
pride. The rebel is older than all the kingdoms he has rebelled
against. There is the lesson of *Cinderella*, which is the same
as the Magnificat–*exaltavit humiles*, or "lifting up the
lowly." There is the great lesson of *Beauty and the Beast*–that
a thing must be loved before it is loveable. There is the frightful parable of *Sleeping Beauty*, which tells how the human

creature was blessed with all kinds of birthday gifts, yet cursed with death, and how death may also be softened to a sleep.

I am not concerned, however, with any of the separate laws of elfland, but with the total essence of its law, which I learned before I could speak, and will keep within me when I can no longer write. I am concerned with a certain way of looking at life. It is a perspective that was created in me by the fairy tales, but since then has been quietly confirmed by the simple facts.

It could be put in this way. There are certain sequences or developments–instances of one thing following another– which are truly reasonable and truly necessary, such as mathematical or simply logical sequences. We creatures of fairyland (who are the most reasonable of all creatures) admit these sequences must be reasonable and necessary. For example, if the Ugly Stepsisters are older than Cinderella, then it is (in a constricting and terrible sense) *necessary* that Cinderella is younger than her sisters. There is just no getting out of it. You may preach all the fatalism you want about that fact, because it really must be true. If Jack is the son of a miller, then a miller is the father of Jack. Cold logic orders it from her awful throne, and we fairylanders submit. If the three brothers all ride horses, then there are six animals and eighteen legs involved. That is true rationalism, and fairyland is full of it.

But as I lifted my head over the wall of the elves and began to take notice of the "real" world, I observed an extraordinary thing. I observed that educated men in glasses were talking about the actual things that happened–dawn and death and things like that–as if they were rational and inevitable, too. They talked as if the fact that trees grow fruit was just as necessary as the fact that two trees plus one tree equals three. But it isn't as necessary. There is a huge difference if you use the test of fairyland, which is the test of the imagination. You can't *imagine* two plus one not equaling three. But you can easily imagine trees not growing fruit. You can, instead, imagine them growing golden candlesticks or tigers hanging on by the tail.

These men in glasses spoke highly of a man named Isaac Newton who was hit by an apple and discovered a law. But we fairylanders couldn't get them to see the distinction between a true law (a law of reason) and the simple fact that apples fall. If the apple hit Newton's nose, then Newton's nose hit the apple. That really is necessary, because we can't imagine one of these happening without the other. But we can quite easily imagine the apple not falling on his nose. We may like to imagine it flying eagerly through the air to hit some other nose that it more passionately disliked. We have always kept this sharp distinction in our fairy tales, the distinction between the science of mental connections (in which there really are laws) and the science of physical facts (in which there aren't any laws, but only weird repetitions). We believe in physical miracles, but not in mental impossibilities. We believe that a bean-stalk climbed up to Heaven, but that doesn't confuse our beliefs at all about the philosophical question of how many beans it takes to make five.

Here is the unexpected but perfect combination of tone and truth in the fairy tales. The people of science say, "Cut down the tree, and the apple will fall." But they say it calmly, as if the first idea really led up to the second. The witch in the fairy tale, however, says, "Blow the horn, and the ogre's castle will fall." But she doesn't say it as if it were something in which the effect obviously resulted from the cause. I am sure she has given that advice to many champions, and she has seen many castles fall, but she doesn't lose either her wonder or her reason. She doesn't stir up her brain until she imagines a necessary mental connection between a horn and a falling castle.

The scientific people, however, do stir their brains until they imagine a necessary mental connection between an apple leaving the tree and an apple hitting the ground. They really do talk as if they have found not only a set of wonderful facts, but also a truth that connects those facts. They really do talk as if the physical connection of two strange things also connect philosophically. They feel that, because one incomprehensible thing constantly follows another incomprehensible thing, the two things somehow combine to make a comprehensible thing. Two black riddles apparently make a white answer.

In fairyland, we avoid the word "law." But in the land of science, they are especially fond of it. They take some interesting idea about how forgotten folks used to pronounce the alphabet and call it "Grimm's Law." But Grimm's Law isn't nearly as intellectual as Grimm's Fairy Tales. Because the tales actually are tales, while the law isn't really a law. The word "law" implies that we know the nature of whatever we are observing, how it is carried out, and how it all works—not merely that we have noticed some of its effects. If there is a law that pick-pockets will go to prison, it implies that we can imagine some connection between the idea of prison and the idea of picking pockets. And we know what that connection is. We can, in fact, explain why we take liberty from a man who takes liberties. But we can't say why an egg can turn into a chicken any more than we can say why a bear could turn into a fairy prince. As *ideas*, the egg and the chicken have a lesser mental connection than the bear and the prince. No egg in and of itself suggests the idea of a chicken, whereas some princes do suggest the idea of bears.

So, now that we know certain transformations do happen, it is essential that we should think of them in the philosophical way of fairy tales, not in the unphilosophical way of science and the "Laws of Nature." When we are asked why eggs turn into birds or why fruits fall in autumn, we must answer exactly as the fairy godmother would answer if Cinderella asked her why mice turned into horses or her clothes fell from her at midnight. We must answer that it is *magic*. We can't call it a "law," because we don't understand its formula. It isn't *required* to happen, because even though we can count on it happening practically, we have no right to say it must *always* happen. The fact that we can bank on things happening like they normally do doesn't prove the existence of unchangeable laws. We don't bank on it. We bet on it. We risk the unlikely chance of a miracle just as we risk the chance of a poisoned pancake or a world-destroying comet. We don't account for that small possibility, not because it is a miracle and therefore impossible, but because it is a miracle and therefore an unlikely exception.

All the terms used in the science books– "law," "necessity," "order," "tendency," and other words like these–are really unintellectual, because they assume we have an inner understanding, which we really don't have. The only words that ever satisfied me when describing Nature are the terms used in the fairy books– "charm," "spell," "enchantment." They express the randomness of the observation and its mystery. A tree grows fruit because it is a *magic* tree. Water runs downhill because it is *bewitched*. The sun shines because it is *enchanted*.

◎ Faith and Fairy Tales ◎

Blessed are the legend-makers with their rhyme
Of things not found within recorded time.
—J.R.R. Tolkien, "Mythopoeia"

Fairy tales and fantasy literature have deep roots in the Christian tradition. The act of conveying timeless truths within a fantastical realm, born from the imagination, echoes God's creative endeavor in bringing *this* world into existence. So, it should come as little surprise that Chesterton, a fervent imaginator, was a champion of fairy tales. In fact, the famous Neil Gaiman credits Chesterton with inspiring him to become a fantasy writer, and in one of his books he quoted Chesterton as saying, "Fairy tales are more than true – not because they tell us dragons exist, but because they tell us dragons can be beaten." But Gaiman is not the only notable writer influenced by Chesterton's foray into fantasy. C.S. Lewis crafted the legendary Aslan and the enchanting world of Narnia, J.R.R. Tolkien's masterpiece, *The Lord of the Rings*, is infused with deeper meaning, and J.K. Rowling admittedly interwove Christian themes into a little book series called *Harry Potter*.

I completely deny that this is fanciful or even mystical. We may have some mysticism later, but this fairy tale language about things is simply rational and agnostic. It is the only way I can express in words how clear and positive I am that one thing is very different than another thing–that there is no logical connection between flying and laying eggs. It is the person who talks about a "law" they have never seen who is the mystic.

Better yet, the ordinary scientific man is rigidly sentimental. He is sentimental in the technical sense of the word because he gets swept away by simple connections of things. He has so often seen birds fly and lay eggs that he feels as if there must be some dreamy, tender connection between the two things, where there really isn't one. A brokenhearted lover might be unable to dissociate the moon from lost love; the materialist is unable to dissociate the moon from the tide. In both cases there is no connection, except that we have seen them together.

A sentimental person might shed a tear at the smell of apple blossom, because, by his own mysterious association, it reminded him of his childhood. Similarly, the materialist professor (though he hides his tears) is also sentimental, because, by his own mysterious association, apple blossoms remind him of apples. But the cool rationalist from fairyland doesn't see why, in theory, the apple tree couldn't grow crimson tulips; where she is from, it sometimes does.

A Pleasant Surprise

This basic wonder toward the world, however, isn't simply a fascination extracted from the fairy tales. On the contrary, all the fire of the fairy tales is extracted from this: just as we all like love stories because they arouse our instinct of sex, we all like fairy tales because they arouse our ancient instinct of astonishment.

This is proven by the fact that when we are very young children, we don't need fairy tales–we only need tales. A simple life is interesting enough. A seven-year-old child is excited to hear that Tommy opened a door and saw a dragon. But a three-year-old is excited to hear that Tommy opened a door. Children like romantic and idyllic stories, but babies like realistic stories, because they see them as romantic. In fact, a baby is about the only person I can think of who wouldn't be bored by reading a modern realistic novel. This proves that even nursery rhymes are only an echo of the interest and amazement we had in the world almost before we were born. These stories tell of apples that are golden only to refresh our memory of when we discovered they were red. These stories make rivers run with wine only to make us remember, if only for one wild moment, that they run with water.

I have said this is completely reasonable and agnostic. And, on this point, I am all for the highest form of agnosticism. The better name for it is Ignorance. You may have heard the story of the man who has forgotten his name. This man walks around town and can see and appreciate everything. The only thing is that he can't remember who he is. Well, every man is that man in the story. Every man has forgotten who he is. A man may understand the universe, but he will never understand the ego; the self is further away than any star. Thou shalt love the Lord thy God, but thou shalt *know* thyself.

We are all victims of the same mental disaster. We have all forgotten our names. We have all forgotten what we really are. All that we call common sense and rationality and practicality and logic only means that, for certain lifeless periods of our life, we forget that we have forgotten. But all that we call spirit and art and ecstasy only means that, for one critical instant, we *remember* that we forget.

Even though (like the man who lost his memory) we walk around town with a weak sense of wonder, it is still wonder. And the wonder has an element of praise to it. This is the next milestone to be marked on our journey through fairyland. In the next chapter, I will speak about the intellectual sides of optimists and pessimists, to the degree that they have one. But here I am only trying to describe the enormous emotions that can't be described. And the strongest emotion was that life was as precious as it was puzzling. It was blissful because it was an adventure; it was an adventure because it was an opportunity. The goodness of the fairy tale wasn't affected by the fact that there might be more dragons than princesses; it was just good to be in a fairy tale.

The test of all happiness is gratitude, and I felt grateful, although I didn't know who to thank. Children are grateful when Santa Claus puts toys or candy in their stockings. Couldn't I be grateful to Santa Claus when he put in my stockings the gift of two miraculous legs? We thank people for birthday presents of cigars and slippers. Can't I thank anyone for the birthday present of birth?

To summarize, I had these first two feelings that I can't defend and no one could attack. First, I felt that the world was a shock. But it was more than just shocking. Existence was a surprise, but I also felt it was a *pleasant* surprise. In fact, all of my first ideas are perfectly stated in a joke that has stuck in my brain since I was a kid. The question was, "What did the first frog say?" And the answer was, "GOD, you made me *jump*!" That says briefly and clearly all that I am trying to say. God made the frog jump, but the frog also prefers jumping.

The Doctrine of Conditional Joy

Now we must move on to the second great principle of the fairy philosophy. Anyone could clearly see this principle in "Grimm's Fairy Tales." For my love of formality, I will call it the Doctrine of Conditional Joy.

Fairy tales talk of great virtue in the conditional word "if." According to elfin ethics, all virtue is in an "if." The attitude of the fairy statement is always, "You may live in a palace of gold and sapphire, *if* you do not say the word 'cow.'" Or, "You may live happily with the King's daughter, *if* you do not show her an onion." The great vision of what could be always hangs upon a veto. All the dizzy and colossal things that are given depend upon one small thing that is held back. All the wild and whirling things that are let loose depend upon one small thing that is forbidden.

Some writers, including Yeats, have described the creatures of fairyland as lawless, dancing about in innocent anarchy all around us. Well, I say these people aren't stupid enough to understand fairyland. Fairies prefer people like me who gape and grin and do what they're told. These writers portray fairies as rebelling against something they know only too well. But the true citizen of fairyland obeys something that he doesn't understand at all.

In the fairy tale, an incomprehensible happiness depends upon an incomprehensible condition. A box is opened, and all evil things fly out. A word is forgotten, and cities crumble. A lamp is lit, and love flies away. A flower is plucked, and human lives are lost. An apple is eaten, and the hope of God is gone.

This is the tone of fairy tales. And I am sure it isn't lawlessness or even freedom. Fairy godmothers seem at least as strict as ordinary godmothers. Cinderella received a carriage from Wonderland and a driver from thin air, but she received a command–which may as well have come from London–that she should be back by twelve. Also, she had a glass slipper, and it can't be a coincidence that glass is so commonly involved in folklore. This princess lives in a glass castle and that princess lives on a glass hill; this one can see all things in a glass mirror; they could all live in glass houses as long as they don't throw any stones.

This thin glitter of glass everywhere expresses the fact that the happiness in fairyland is bright but brittle, just like that substance that could very easily be broken by a housemaid or a cat. And this fairy-tale feeling sank into me and became my feeling toward the whole world. I felt (and feel) that life itself is as bright as a diamond, but as brittle as a windowpane. And when I read where Ezekiel compared the heavens to a gleaming crystal, I can remember that I trembled. I was afraid God would drop the cosmos with a crash.

Remember, however, that "breakable" isn't the same as "perishable." Strike a piece of glass, and it won't last a second. But don't strike it, and it will last a thousand years. The joy of man, it seemed, was just like this, either in elfland or on earth. The happiness depended on not doing something which you could choose to do at any moment, and which usually wasn't obvious as to why you shouldn't do it.

Now, the point here, to me, is that this didn't seem unfair. If the miller's third son said to the fairy, "Explain why I shouldn't stand on my head in the fairy palace," the fairy might justly reply, "Well, if we are going to go there, then explain the fairy palace." If Cinderella says, "Why is it that I must leave the ball at twelve?" her godmother might answer, "Why is it that you get to be there until twelve?" If I put a man in my will and leave him ten talking elephants and a hundred winged horses, he shouldn't complain if the conditions of the will match the slight eccentricity of the gift. He shouldn't look a winged horse in the mouth.

It seemed to me that existence itself was a wildly eccentric inheritance. I couldn't complain about the seemingly arbitrary limitations of the gift when I didn't understand the gift they limited. The frame was no stranger than the picture itself. The veto might be as wild as the vision; it might be as shocking as the sun, as mysterious as the waters, as fanciful and ferocious as the towering trees.

For this reason (let's call it the fairy godmother philosophy) I never could participate with the young people of my generation in what they called the general feeling of revolt. Let's hope I resisted any rules that were evil, and I'll deal with these evil rules in another chapter, but I didn't feel inclined to resist any rule just because I couldn't understand it. Property rights are sometimes exchanged in foolish ways simply to satisfy the legal system, like the breaking of a stick or the payment of a penny. I was willing to hold the rights to the huge estate of earth and Heaven by any silly means as this. It couldn't possibly be wilder than the fact I got to hold the rights at all.

At this point I will give only one ethical example to explain what I mean. I could never join in with the popular buzz from my generation about attacking monogamy, because no restriction on sex seemed as odd and unexpected as sex itself. To be allowed, like the Greek hero Endymion, to make love to the moon and then complain that Jupiter kept his own moons for himself seemed to me (who was bred on fairy tales like Endymion's) to be tastelessly anti-climactic. Faithfulness to one woman is a small price to pay for so much as seeing one woman. To complain that I could only be married once was like complaining that I had only been born once. It was out of proportion with the awesome excitement of the thing. It didn't show an exaggerated appreciation for sex, but rather an exaggerated *lack* of appreciation. Only a fool would complain that he can't enter Eden through five gates at once. Polygamy is not realizing what sex really is. It is like absent-mindedly plucking five pears at once.

There have been lovers of beauty who stretched the limits of language to write insane tributes to the lovely things. A tree leaf made them weep; a particularly shiny beetle brought them to their knees. And yet their emotion never impressed me for a second, because it never occurred to them to pay for their pleasure with any sort of symbolic sacrifice. I felt that people should fast forty days just to hear a blackbird sing. They should walk through fire to find a flower. Yet these lovers of beauty couldn't even keep sober to hear the blackbird. They wouldn't go through with a common Christian marriage as a way to earn the boutonniere on their lapel. Surely a person might pay for extraordinary joy with ordinary morals.

A Collision with the Modern World

Well, I left the fairy tales lying on the floor of the nursery, and I haven't found any book as sensible since. I left my nanny–the guardian of tradition and democracy–and I haven't found any modern type of person as sanely radical or as sanely conservative. But the most important thing to note was this: when I first went out into the intellectual atmosphere of the modern world, I found that the modern world was exactly opposed to my nanny and to the fairy tales. It has taken me a long time to discover that the modern world is wrong, and my nanny was right.

The really interesting thing was that modern thought contradicted this basic belief of my boyhood on two of its most important doctrines. I have explained that the fairy tales built two attitudes in me. First, that this world is a wild and surprising place, a place that could have been very different but is actually very lovely. And second, that when enjoying this wildness and loveliness, we should be modest and submit to the strangest restrictions of a strange kindness. But I found the whole modern world running like a high tide against both of these feelings of mine. The aftermath of this collision created in me two sudden and spontaneous reactions. I have felt these things ever since, and they have gradually turned from raw ideas into hardened convictions.

Monotony and the Magician

First, I found the whole modern world consumed by scientific fatalism, saying that everything is as it always had to have been, being perfectly unfolded from the beginning of time. The leaf on the tree is green because it could never have been anything else. But the fairy-tale philosophers are glad that the leaf is green exactly because it could have been scarlet. They feel as if it had turned green an instant before they looked at it. They are pleased that snow is white for the purely reasonable reason that it might have been black. Every color has a bold quality to it, as if the color had been *chosen*. The red of garden roses seems not only like a decision but also a drama, like suddenly spilt blood. They feel as if something has been *done*.

The great determinists of the nineteenth century, however, were strongly against this natural feeling that something had happened an instant before. In fact, according to them, nothing had every really happened since the beginning of time. Nothing had ever happened since existence had happened, and they weren't even sure about when *that* happened.

The modern world as I saw it was sold on predestination and modern Calvinism, and how inevitable it was that things turned out as they had. But when I asked them about this, I found they really had no proof of this unavoidable repetition in things, except for the fact that things were repeated. This simple repetition, however, made the things more unusual to me rather than more rational. It was as if I had seen a man with an oddly shaped nose and dismissed it as simply unfortunate, then seen six other noses with the same surprising shape. I would have thought for a moment that it must have been some local secret society. Similarly, I thought one elephant having a trunk was odd, but all elephants having trunks looked like a conspiracy.

I am only speaking here of an emotion—an emotion both stubborn and subtle. And this repetition in Nature sometimes seemed to be an *enthusiastic* repetition, like an angry schoolteacher saying the same thing over and over again. The grass seemed to be signaling to me with all its fingers at once; the crowded stars seemed determined to be understood. The sun would make me see him even if he had to rise a thousand times. The repetitions of the universe began to feel like the maddening rhythm of a mysterious chant, and I began to see an idea.

All lofty materialism that dominates the modern mind ultimately rests upon one assumption, and it is a false assumption. It is assumed that if a thing goes on repeating itself, then it is probably dead, like a piece of clockwork. Some people feel that if the universe was personal, then its behaviors would vary, and if the sun were alive it would dance. This is false even in relation to things we know about. Variation in human activity, for example, is not brought about by life, but by death, because our strength and desire are dying down. A man varies his behavior because of some kind of failure or fatigue. He gets into a taxi because he is tired of walking, or he walks because he is tired of sitting still. But if his life and joy were so gigantic that he never got tired of going to Islington, then he might go to Islington as regularly as the River Thames goes downstream to Sheerness. The speed and bliss of his life would look like the stillness of death. The sun rises every morning, but I don't rise every morning. My varying behavior isn't due to my activity, however, but to my lack of activity. To use a popular phrase, it might be true that the sun rises every day because he never gets tired of rising. His routine might be due, not to a lifelessness, but to a rush of life.

What I am trying to explain can be seen, for example, in children, when they find some game or joke they especially enjoy. A child kicks his legs rhythmically because he has too much life, not a lack of life. It is because children have abundant energy, because they are fierce and free in spirit, that they want things repeated and unchanged. They always say, "Do it again," and the grown-up person does it again until he is nearly dead. Grown-up people aren't strong enough to exult in monotony. But maybe God *is* strong enough to exult in monotony.

It is possible that God says every morning, "Do it again" to the sun. And every evening, "Do it again" to the moon. Maybe it is not necessary that all daisies be alike. Maybe God makes every daisy separately but has never gotten tired of making them. Maybe God has the eternal appetite of infancy–for we have sinned and grown old, and our Father is younger than we.

Maybe the repetition in Nature isn't a simple reoccurrence; maybe it is a theatrical *encore*. Maybe Heaven gave an encore to the bird who laid an egg. If the human being becomes pregnant and gives birth to a human child instead of a fish, or a bat, or a griffin, maybe the reason is not that we are trapped in an animal destiny without life or purpose. Instead, maybe our sad little play has touched the gods, that they admire it from their starry balcony, and that at the end of every human opera, humanity is called again and again to sing encore after encore. Repetition may be chosen to go on for millions of years, and at any moment it may stop. Humans may stand on the earth generation after generation, and yet each newborn baby be their absolutely last appearance.

This was my first conviction, made by the shock of my childish emotions colliding with modern thought. I had always vaguely felt the real things of the world to be miracles in the sense that they were wonderful. Now I began to think of them as miracles in the more technical sense that they were *willful*. What I mean is that they were, or might be, repeated decisions of some will.

To put it simply, I had always believed that the world involved magic. Now I thought that it may involve a magician. And this pointed to a profound emotion that had always been present and subconscious. I had always felt that this world of ours has a purpose, and if there is a purpose, there is a person. I felt that life was primarily a story, and if there is a story, there is a storyteller.

Limits and the Size of the Universe

Modern thought also collided with my second belief. It went against the fairy feeling about strict limits and conditions. The one thing moderns loved to talk about was expansion and largeness. Herbert Spencer popularized this despicable idea that the size of the solar system should overpower the spiritual beliefs of man. But why should a man surrender his self-worth to the solar system any more than to a whale? If it is simply the size of man that proves he is not the image of God, then a whale could be the image of God, although it would be a somewhat formless image; you could even call the image an impressionist portrait. It is quite useless to argue that man is small compared to the cosmos, because man has always been small compared to the nearest tree. But these moderns, in their reckless imperialism, would say that we had in some way been conquered and taken prisoner by the astronomical universe. They turned all of mankind into a small, colonized nation.

The expansion I am referring to, however, is much more evil than all this. I have stated that the materialist, like the madman, is in prison—the prison of one thought. These people seemed to think it was exceptionally inspiring to keep on saying the prison was very large. But the size of this scientific universe gave no one anything fresh to relieve them from their boredom.

The cosmos went on forever, but not even in its wildest constellation could there be anything really interesting–anything, for instance, such as forgiveness or free will. The fact that it was endless added nothing to it. It was like telling a prisoner in jail that he would be happy to hear that the jail now covered half the country. The warden would have nothing to show the man except more and more long hallways of stone lit by frightful lights and empty of all that is human. Similarly, these expanders of the universe had nothing to show us except more and more infinite hallways of outer space lit by frightful suns and empty of all that is divine.

In fairyland there had been a real law. It was a law that could be broken. That is the definition of a law–something that can be broken. But the machinery of this cosmic prison was something that couldn't be broken because we ourselves were just a part of its machinery. We were either never going to do things or we were always destined to do them. The doctrine of conditional joy was nowhere to be found. We can have neither the comfort of following laws nor the fun of breaking them. The largeness of this universe didn't have any of that freshness and airiness that we praised in the universe of the poet. This modern universe is literally an empire. It is an empire because it is huge, but not free. A man could walk into larger and larger windowless rooms, rooms as big as Babylon, but he could never find the smallest window or a breath of fresh air.

These hellish parallels seemed to grow with distance, but for me, all good things come to a point, like swords. So, when I found that huge universe to be so disappointing, I began to argue about it a little, and soon I found that the whole thing was shallower than I could have imagined. According to these people, the universe was *one thing* since it had one un-broken rule. But they would say that while it is one thing, it is also the *only* thing. So why, then, should we call this one thing large? There is nothing to compare it to. It would make just as much sense to call it small. A person may say, "I like this huge cosmos, with its sea of stars and its multitude of varied creatures." But if it comes to that, why shouldn't they say, "I like this cozy little cosmos, with its decent number of stars and as tidy a supply of livestock as I want to see"? One is just as good as the other. They are both simply opinions.

It is an emotional reaction to rejoice that the sun is larger than the earth; it is just as sane a reaction to rejoice that the sun isn't any bigger than it is. A person chooses to have an emotion about the largeness of the world; why shouldn't he choose to have an emotion about its smallness? It just so happened that I had that emotion.

When someone takes a liking to anything, they think of it as a smaller version of itself, even if it is an elephant or a royal guardsman. The reason for this is that anything, no matter how huge, that can be conceived of as complete, can also be conceived of as small. If military mustaches didn't make you think of a sword and if tusks didn't suggest a tail, then the object would be too enormous to be measured. But the moment you imagine a *whole* guardsman, you can imagine a *small* guardsman. The moment you really see an elephant, you can name it "Tiny." If you can make a statue of a thing, you can make a statuette of it.

These people claimed that the universe was one united thing, but they didn't like this universe. I, however, was very fond of the universe and wanted to think of it as a very small thing. I often did think of it like this, and it didn't seem to mind. Honestly and truthfully, I felt that my vague beliefs about abounding life were better expressed by calling the world small than by calling it large, because the idea of infinity had a sort of carelessness that was the opposite of the fierce and reverent caution I felt touching the pricelessness and peril of life.

These people felt the world was only a boring waste. I felt it was a sort of sacred and careful thrift. Frugality is much more romantic than extravagance. To them the stars were an unending income of pennies. But I felt the same about the golden sun and the silver moon as a schoolboy feels if he has one gold coin and one silver.

Saved from a Wreck

These subconscious convictions are best characterized by the color and tone of certain stories. I have already said that stories of magic alone can express my feeling that life isn't only a pleasure, but also a kind of eccentric privilege. I will express this other feeling of a small cosmic coziness, then, by referencing another book that children read, *Robinson Crusoe*. I read this book at about the same time I began to feel these things, and it owes its eternal shelf life to the fact that it celebrates the poetry of limitations, or better yet, the wild romance of prudence.

Crusoe is a man on a small rock with a few comforts he snatched from the sea. The best thing in the book is simply the list of things he saved from the wreck. The greatest of poems is an inventory list. Every kitchen utensil becomes the *perfect* utensil because it could have been lost in the sea. It is a good exercise, in the empty or boring hours of the day, to look at anything, maybe the oven mitt or the bookcase, and think about how happy someone could be to have saved it from the sinking ship and dragged it onto the lonely island. But it is an even better exercise to remember how *all* things have had this split-second escape. Everything has been saved from a wreck. Every person has had at least one horrible adventure. It is the same adventure they wouldn't have survived if the birth were untimely, the same adventure as babies who have never seen the light. As a child, I heard people speak often about ruined men of genius, and it was common to say that many a person was a Great Might-Have-Been. But to me, it was more solid and stunning to think that any person in town was a Great Might-*Not*-Have-Been.

I really felt (this may sound silly) as if the exact order and number of things were the romantic remains of Crusoe's ship. That there are two sexes and one sun was like the fact that there were two guns and one axe. It was urgent that we shouldn't lose one. But somehow, it was a little fun that we couldn't add one, either. The trees and the planets seemed like things saved from the wreck, and when I saw the Alps, I was glad they hadn't been lost in the confusion. I felt careful not to waste the stars as if they were sapphires. I hoarded the hills. The universe is a single jewel, and while we often talk of a jewel as peerless and priceless, it is literally true of this jewel. This cosmos really is without peer and without price, because there can't be another one.

A Rough Summary

Like this I end, in unavoidable inadequacy, my attempt to describe the indescribable. These are my ultimate attitudes toward life, and they make good soils for the seeds of doctrine. I thought these things, in some mysterious way, before I could write, and I felt them before I could think. And so that we can carry on more easily after this, I will roughly summarize.

First, I felt in my bones that the world doesn't explain itself. Maybe it is a miracle with a supernatural explanation, or maybe the magic is only an illusion with a natural explanation. But the explanation of the illusion will have to be better than the natural explanations I have heard if it is going to satisfy me. The thing is magic. That is either true or false.

Second, I came to feel as if magic must have a meaning, and meaning must have someone to mean it. There was something personal in the world, as in a work of art; whatever it meant, it meant violently.

Third, I thought the design of this purpose was beautiful, even despite its imperfections, such as dragons.

Fourth, that the proper way to say thanks to it was some form of humility and restraint. We should thank God for beer and Burgundy by not drinking too much of them. We owed, also, an obedience to whatever made us.

Last, and strangest of all, there had come into my mind a vague and sweeping impression that there had been some ancient ruin, and in some way all good was a remnant to be stored and held sacred. Man had saved his good just as Crusoe saved his goods. He had saved them from a wreck.

All of this I felt, and my generation didn't encourage me to feel it. And all this time I hadn't even thought of Christian theology.

5
The Flag of the World

When I was a boy there were two peculiar kinds of people who we called optimists and pessimists. I constantly used those words myself, but I will happily admit that I never really knew what they meant. The only obvious thing was that these words couldn't mean what people said they meant.

The usual explanation was that the optimist considered the world to be as good as it could be, while the pessimist considered it as bad as it could be. As both of these statements were obviously raving nonsense, I had to go looking for other explanations. An optimist couldn't mean someone who thought everything right and nothing wrong, because that is meaningless; it is like calling everything right and nothing left. Ultimately, I concluded that the optimist considered everything good except the pessimist, and that the pessimist considered everything bad except himself.

It would be unfair to leave out from this list of definitions the mysterious but insightful one said to have been given by a little girl: "An optimist is someone who looks after your eyes, and a pessimist is someone who looks after your feet." This may be the best definition of all. There is even a sort of hidden meaning in it, because it may help us distinguish between that more dreary thinker who considers only our contact with the earth from moment to moment, and that happier thinker who focuses instead on our primary ability to see and choose a path.

This alternative of the optimist and the pessimist is a terrible mistake, however. The assumption here is that we should criticize the world as if we were house hunting, as if we were being shown a new suite of apartments. If a man came to this world from some other world, he might discuss whether the advantage of summer woods made up for the disadvantage of rabid dogs, just as a man looking for a house might weigh the presence of a balcony against the absence of an ocean view. But no one is in that position. We belong to this world before we begin to ask if it is nice to belong to it. We have fought for the flag of our country, and often won heroic victories for the flag, long before we ever enlisted. To put it simply, we have a loyalty to the world long before we have any admiration for it.

Patriotism: The Source of Creative Energy

In the last chapter I said that my primary feeling toward the world–that it is strange and yet attractive–is best expressed by fairy tales. The reader may, if they like, attribute the next stage of my life to that aggressive and even militant literature which often comes next in the history of a boy. We can all credit much of our sound morality to comic books.

For whatever reason, it seemed and still seems to me that a better attitude toward life can be expressed in terms of a kind of military loyalty than in the usual terms of criticism and approval. My acceptance of the universe is not optimism. It is more like patriotism. It is a matter of where my loyalty lies. The world isn't a room I could rent in Brighton, a room I could leave because it is miserable. Instead, it is the fortress of our family, with the flag flying on the tower, and the more miserable it is, the less we should leave it.

The point is not that the world is too sad to love or too glad not to love; the point is that when you do love something, its gladness is a reason for loving it, and its sadness is a reason for loving it even more. All optimistic thoughts about England and all pessimistic thoughts about her are all reasons for the English patriot to love England. Similarly, all optimism about the cosmos and all pessimism about her are all arguments for the cosmic patriot to love the cosmos.

Let's say we are dealing with a desperate, miserable thing—say the area of Pimlico in central London. If we think about what is really best for Pimlico, we will find that this train of thought leads to mystic patriotism. It isn't enough for a man to disapprove of Pimlico. In that case he will simply cut his throat or move to Chelsea. And it certainly isn't enough for a man to approve of Pimlico, because then it will remain Pimlico, which would be awful. The only way out of it seems to be for somebody to *love* Pimlico, to love it with a transcendental connection and without any earthly reason.

If a person who truly loved Pimlico existed, then Pimlico would raise herself into ivory towers and golden pinnacles. Pimlico would dress herself as a woman does when she's loved. Decoration isn't given to hide horrible things. They are given to decorate things already adorable. A mother doesn't give her child a pink bow because she is very ugly without it. A lover doesn't give a woman a necklace to hide her neck. If men loved Pimlico as mothers loved children, if they loved it arbitrarily, simply because it is theirs, Pimlico in a year or two might be more beautiful than Florence.

Some readers will say this is just a fantasy. My answer is that this is the actual history of mankind. It is a fact that this is how cities grew great. Go back to the darkest roots of civilization, and you will find them gathered around some sacred stone or encircling some sacred well. People first paid honor to a spot and then afterwards gained glory for it. Men didn't love Rome because she was great. She was great because they loved her.

The eighteenth-century theories of the social contract—the idea that the origin of morality was an agreement among individuals to give up some personal freedoms in order to gain the benefits of the community—have been exposed to plenty of clumsy criticism in our time. These theories were clearly right to the extent that they meant there is an idea of contentment and cooperation at the root of all government throughout history. But they really were wrong to the extent they suggested people had ever directly aimed at order or ethics by a conscious give and take of benefits.

Morality didn't begin by one person saying to another, "I will not hit you if you do not hit me." There isn't any record of that conversation. But there is a record of both men having said, "We must not hit each other in the holy place." They gained their morality by guarding their religion. They didn't cultivate courage for the sake of courage. They fought for the shrine, and then found they had become courageous. They didn't cultivate cleanliness for the sake of cleanliness. They purified themselves for the altar, and then found that they were clean.

The history of the Jews is the only early document known to most Englishmen, and the historical facts can be judged well enough from that. The Ten Commandments, which are for the most part common to mankind, were simply military commands–a code of regimental orders issued to protect a certain holy ark across a certain desert. In this case, anarchy was evil because it endangered the holiness. And only when they made a holy day for God did they find they had made a holiday for men.

An Unreasonable Loyalty

If we can agree that this foremost commitment to a place or thing leads to creative energy, we can move on to a very peculiar fact. Let's repeat for a moment that the only correct optimism is a kind of universal patriotism. What is the matter, then, with the pessimist? I think it can be stated by saying he is the cosmic anti-patriot. And what is the matter with the anti-patriot? I think it can be stated, without too much bitterness, by saying that he is the honest friend. And what is the matter with the honest friend? Here is where we strike the rock of real life and unchangeable human nature.

I venture to say that what is bad in the honest friend is simply that he is not honest. He keeps something back, and that thing is his own gloomy pleasure in saying unpleasant things. He has a secret desire to hurt, and not simply to help. This is, I think, what makes a particular kind of anti-patriot irritating to healthy citizens.

I am not talking (of course) of the anti-patriotism that is really only patriotism speaking plainly. Anyone who says that no patriot should criticize a war until it is over isn't worth an intelligent answer. They are saying that no good son should warn his mother off a cliff until she has fallen over it.

There is an anti-patriot, however, who honestly angers honest people, and he can be explained, I think, by what I have suggested. He is the *dishonest* honest friend. He is the man who says, "I'm sorry to say we are doomed," and is not sorry at all. And he may be called, without exaggeration, a traitor. He uses that ugly knowledge, which he is allowed to have in order to strengthen the army, to discourage people from joining it. Exactly in the same way, the pessimist (who is the cosmic anti-patriot) uses the freedom that life allows to lead people away from its flag. Even if he states only facts, it is still essential to know his emotions and motives. It may be true that twelve hundred people in Tottenham are down with smallpox, but we want to know whether this is stated only by a common minister who wants to help those people or by some great philosopher who wants to curse the gods.

The evil of the pessimist, then, isn't that he chastises gods and men, but that he doesn't love what he chastises. He doesn't have this foremost and supernatural loyalty to things. And what is the evil of the man usually called an optimist? It is obvious that the optimist, who wants to defend the honor of this world, will defend the indefensible. He will say, "This is my cosmos, and I don't care if it is right or wrong." He will be less inclined to improve things and more inclined to a sort of political and dismissive answer to any criticism, soothing everyone with empty words. He won't wash the world, he will only *whitewash* it.

All of this (which is true about a kind of optimist) leads us to the one really interesting point of psychology which couldn't be explained without it. We say there must be a foremost loyalty to life. The only question, then, is this: will it be a natural or a supernatural loyalty? If you want to think of it this way, will it be a reasonable or an unreasonable loyalty? Now, the extraordinary thing is that this *bad* optimism (the whitewashing, the weak defense of everything) is connected to the *reasonable* optimism. Rational optimism leads to a lack of activity. It is irrational optimism that leads to reform.

Let me explain by once more using the parallel of patriotism. The man who is most likely to ruin a place he loves is exactly the man who loves it *with* a reason. The man who will improve the place is the man who loves it *without* a reason. If a man loves some feature of Pimlico (which seems unlikely), he may find himself defending that feature even in the face of Pimlico itself. But if he simply loves Pimlico itself, he may tear it down and turn it into the paradise of New Jerusalem.

I don't deny there can be too much reform; I only say that it is the mystic patriot who reforms. The complacent kind of patriotism is most common among those who have some specific reason for their patriotism. The worst patriots don't love England, but only a theory of England. If we love England for being an empire, we may overestimate our success in ruling India. But if we love it only for being a nation, we can face anything, because it would be a nation even if India ruled us.

Because of this, only those people whose patriotism depends on history will allow their patriotism to falsify history. A man who loves England simply for being England won't mind how she came about. But a man who loves England for being Anglo-Saxon may go against all the facts just to suit his own tastes. He may declare (like some recent writers) that the

Norman Conquest of England in the 11th century was actually a Saxon Conquest. His argument may end in complete unreason–because he has a reason.

A man who loves France for its military will try to cover up the army of 1870 and its embarrassing defeat. But a man who loves France simply for being France will *improve* the army of 1870. This is exactly what the French have done, and France is a good example of this working paradox. Nowhere else is patriotism as purely abstract and without reason, and nowhere else is reform more drastic and sweeping. The more mystical your patriotism, the more practical your politics.

Maybe the most everyday example of this point is in the case of women and their strange and strong loyalty. Some stupid people started the idea that women are blind and don't see clearly because they support their husbands through everything. These people must not have met any women. The same women who are ready to defend their man through thick and thin are (in their personal relationship with the man) almost disturbingly articulate about the thinness of his excuses or the thickness of his head.

A man's friend likes him but leaves him as he is. His wife loves him and is always trying to turn him into somebody else. She underrates his virtue yet overrates his value. Women who are completely mystic in their beliefs are completely cynical in their criticisms. The enthusiast is entirely free to criticize, and the fanatic can safely be a skeptic.

Love is not blind. That is the last thing it is. Love is *bound*. And the more it is bound, the less it is blind.

The Incurable Romantic

Though Chesterton writes here of how love is bound, his love for his wife Frances had a helping of youthful blindness, too. In a letter Gilbert penned to Frances, he reveals that he fell in love with her at first sight. Reflecting on the night they met, he wrote, "Once in the course of conversation you looked straight at me and I said to myself as plainly as if I had read it in a book: 'If I had anything to do with this girl I should go on my knees to her: if I spoke with her she would never deceive me: if I depended on her she would never deny me: if I loved her she would never play with me: if I trusted her she would never go back on me: if I remembered her she would never forget me." Later in the letter, he wrote, "There are four lamps of thanksgiving always before me. The first is for my creation out of the same earth with such a woman as you. The second is that I have not, with all my faults, 'gone after strange women.' You cannot think how a man's self-restraint is rewarded in this. The third is that I have tried to love everything alive: a dim preparation for loving you. And the fourth is – but no words can express that. Here ends my previous existence. Take it: it led me to you."

Radical Optimism and Radical Pessimism

So, this came to be my position about optimism, pessimism, and improvement: before any cosmic act of reform, we must have a cosmic oath of allegiance. As Proverbs says, "My son, give me thy heart." The heart must be fixed on the right thing. The moment we have a fixed heart, we have a free hand.

I need to pause here to address an obvious criticism. It will be said that a rational person accepts the world as a mixture of good and evil, with a decent amount of satisfaction and a decent amount of tolerance. But this is exactly the attitude that I am saying is defective. This attitude, I know, is very common these days. It was put perfectly in those piercingly blasphemous lines of the English poet Matthew Arnold:

> *Enough we live–and if a life,*
> *With large results so little rife,*
> *Though bearable, seem hardly worth*
> *This pomp of worlds, this pain of birth.*

I know this attitude fills our generation, and I think it freezes our generation. For our Titanic missions of faith and revolution, what we need isn't the cold acceptance of the world as a compromise. Instead, we need some way in which we can wholeheartedly hate and wholeheartedly love it. We don't want joy and anger to neutralize each other and create a sulky contentment. We want a fiercer delight and a fiercer dissatisfaction. We must see the universe as an ogre's castle to be stormed, and yet, at the same time, as our own cottage to which we can come back at night.

No one doubts that an ordinary man can make it in this world, but we don't demand enough strength just to make it, but enough strength to make the world. Can we hate it enough to change it, and yet love it enough to consider it worth changing? Can we look up at its immense good without ever simply accepting it as it is? Can we look up at its immense evil without ever feeling despair? Can we, to put it briefly, be not only a pessimist and an optimist, but be both a *radical* pessimist and a *radical* optimist? Can we be pagan enough to die *for* the world and Christian enough to die *to* it? In this combination of things, I propose, it is the rational optimist who fails, and the irrational optimist who succeeds. He is ready to destroy the whole universe for the sake of itself.

I write these things not in a mature, logical sequence, but as they came to me. And this view of mine was cleared and sharpened by a coincidence that happened around that time. An idea arose under the growing shadow of a playwright named Ibsen, who wrote a character that referred to suicide as "beautiful." People were talking then about whether it was quite nice to murder oneself. Dark modern thinkers told us that we shouldn't even say "poor guy" of a man who had blown his brains out, since he was an enviable person, and had only blown them out because of their exceptional excellence. One critic even suggested that in the golden future there would be slot machines where a man could kill himself for a penny.

In all of this, I found myself completely opposed to many of those who called themselves liberal or humane. Not only is suicide a sin, but it is *the* sin. It is the ultimate and absolute evil, the refusal to take an interest in existence–the refusal to take the oath of loyalty to life. The man who kills a man, kills a man. But the man who kills himself kills *all* men; as far as he is concerned, he wipes out the world. His act is worse (theoretically speaking) than any rape or terrorism. It destroys all buildings, it abuses all women.

The thief is satisfied with diamonds, but the man who commits suicide isn't satisfied. That is his crime. He can't be bribed, even by the blazing crystals of the Celestial City. The thief compliments the things he steals, even if he doesn't compliment the owner of them. But the suicide insults everything on earth by not stealing it. He desecrates every flower by refusing to live for its sake. There is not a tiny creature in the cosmos that isn't sneered at by his death. When a man hangs himself from a tree, the leaves might fall off in anger and the birds fly away in a fury, because both have been personally offended.

Of course, there may be emotional excuses for the action. There often are excuses for rape, and there almost always are for terrorism. Until the 1820's, it was common to mock a suicidal corpse by staking it through the heart and burying it at a crossroads. But if we are talking about clear ideas and intelligent thinking, then there is much more rational and philosophic truth in burying self-murderers at the crossroads and driving a stake through the body than in automatic suicide slot machines. There is meaning in burying the suicidal man apart from others. The man's crime is different from other crimes because it makes even crime impossible.

Around the same time, I read a ridiculous statement by some free thinker who wrote seriously that a man committing suicide was only the same thing as a martyr. The obvious falsehood in this helped to clarify everything for me. Obviously, a suicide is the opposite of a martyr. A martyr is a person who cares so much for something outside themselves that they forget their own personal life. A suicide is a person who cares so little for anything outside themselves that they don't want to see anything ever again. One wants something to begin, the other wants everything to end. In other words, the martyr is noble because, in whatever way they renounce the world or curse humanity, they proclaim this ultimate connection with life. They set their heart outside themselves; they die that something may live. The suicide, however, is not noble because they don't have this connection with life. They are simply a destroyer. Spiritually, they destroy the universe.

Then I remembered the stake and the crossroads, and the odd fact that Christianity had shown this odd harshness to suicide but had shown a wild encouragement of the martyr. Historically, Christianity has been accused of carrying martyrdom and self-denial too far to a place of bleakness and pessimism. The early Christian martyrs talked about death with a horrible happiness. They blasphemed the beautiful jobs of the human body. The far-off grave smelt to them like a field of flowers. All this has seemed to many to be the very poetry of pessimism. Yet there is the stake at the crossroads to show what Christianity really thought of the pessimist. This was the first of the long train of puzzling things with which Christianity entered the discussion. And along with this came something unusual that I will have to speak to more significantly as it applies to all Christian ideas, but which distinctly began in this idea of suicide and martyrdom.

The Christian attitude toward the martyr and the suicide wasn't what is so often portrayed in modern morals. It wasn't a matter of degree. It wasn't that a line must be drawn somewhere, and that the praise-worthy self-slayer fell *within* the line and the sad self-slayer fell just outside it. Evidently the Christian attitude wasn't simply that the suicide was carrying martyrdom too far. The Christian attitude was intensely for one and intensely against the other. These two things that looked so much alike were at opposite ends of Heaven and Hell. One individual threw away their life–they were so good that their dry bones could heal cities from the plague. Another individual threw away life–they were so bad that their bones would pollute their family's bones.

I am not saying this ferocity was right, but why was it so fierce? Here is where I first found that my wandering feet were following a beaten path. Christianity had also felt suicide and martyrdom were opposites. Had it perhaps felt it for the same reason? Had Christianity felt what I felt, but couldn't (and can't) express–this need for a foremost loyalty to things, and then for a devastating reform of things?

Then I remembered that the accusation against Christianity was that it combined these two things which I was wildly trying to combine. Christianity was accused, all at the same time, of being too optimistic about the universe and of being too pessimistic about the world. The coincidence made me suddenly stand still.

The Answer to Optimism and Pessimism

An idiotic pattern has emerged of saying such and such a thing can be believed in one age but can't be believed in another. Some dogma, we are told, was reasonable in the twelfth century, but is not reasonable in the twentieth. You might as well say a certain philosophy can be believed on Mondays but can't be believed on Tuesdays. You might as well say a view of the cosmos is suitable to half past three but isn't suitable to half past four. What a man can believe depends upon his philosophy, not upon the clock or the century. If a man believes in unchangeable natural laws, then he can't believe in any miracle, in any age. If a man believes in a will that governs those laws, he can believe in any miracle, in any age.

Let's suppose, for the sake of argument, we take the case of miraculous healing. A materialist of the twelfth century couldn't believe it any more than a materialist of the twentieth century. But a Christian of the twentieth century can believe in miraculous healing as much as a Christian of the twelfth century. It is simply a matter of a person's theory of things. So, when dealing with any historical answer to a question, the point isn't whether it was given in our time, but whether it was given in response to the question. And the more I thought about when and how Christianity came into the world, the more I felt it came to answer this question of optimism and pessimism.

Now, it is usually the loose and broad-minded Christians who pay indefensible compliments to Christianity. They talk as if there had never been any reverence or compassion until Christianity came, which is a point that any medieval person would have been eager to correct. They state that the remarkable thing about Christianity was that it was the first to preach simplicity or self-control, or inwardness and sincerity. They will think I am very close-minded (whatever that means) if I say the remarkable thing about Christianity was that it was the first *to preach Christianity*. Its peculiarity was that it was peculiar. Simplicity and sincerity are not peculiar, but instead obvious ideals for all mankind. Christianity was the answer to a riddle, not the last, obvious truth uttered at the end of a long speech. Let me explain.

The Worship of the God Within

Only the other day I saw something in a Puritan newspaper that said Christianity, when stripped of its armor of dogma (as if a man could be stripped of his armor of bones), turned out to be nothing but the Quaker doctrine of the "Inner Light." Now, if I were to say that Christianity came into the world specifically to destroy the doctrine of the Inner Light, then that would be an exaggeration. But it would be much closer to the truth than what that newspaper claimed. The last Stoics, like Roman emperor Marcus Aurelius, were the exact people who believed in the Inner Light. Their dignity, their weariness, their sad outward care for others, and their incurable internal care for themselves all came from the Inner Light and existed only because of that dismal illumination.

Notice that Marcus Aurelius teaches, as these introspective teachers of morality always do, about *small* things done or not done. It is because he doesn't have enough hate or love to make a large moral revolution. He wakes up very early in the morning, just as our own rich aristocrats living the Simple Life get up early in the morning, because this kind of generosity is much easier than stopping the gladiator games of the colosseum or giving the English people back their land. Marcus Aurelius is the most intolerable of human types. He is an unselfish egoist. An unselfish egoist is a man who is prideful without the excuse of passion.

Of all the imaginable forms of enlightenment, the worst is what these people call the Inner Light. Of all horrible religions, the most horrible is the worship of the god within. Anyone who knows anybody knows how this would work. To say that Mr. Jones worships the god within ultimately turns out to mean that Jones worships Jones. Let Jones worship the sun or moon, anything but the Inner Light. Let Jones worship cats or crocodiles if he can find any in his street, but not the god within.

Christianity first came into the world to violently assert that a man didn't only have to look inside himself but could look *outside* himself–to behold with astonishment and enthusiasm a divine army and a divine captain. The only fun of being a Christian was that a person wasn't left alone with the Inner Light, but instead recognized an outer light, fair as the sun, clear as the moon, frightful as an army with banners.

The Unnatural Worship of Nature

At the same time, it will be good if Jones doesn't worship the sun and moon. If he does, there will be a tendency for him to imitate them, to say that he may burn insects alive because the sun burns insects alive. He thinks that because the sun gives people sunstroke, he may give his neighbors the measles. He thinks that because the moon is said to drive people crazy, he may drive his wife crazy.

This ugly side of simple outward optimism showed itself in the ancient world. About the time when the Stoic idealism began to show the weaknesses of pessimism, the old nature worship of the ancients began to show the enormous weaknesses of optimism. Nature worship is natural enough while a society is young. Or, in other words, Pantheism is alright as long as it is the worship of the goat-god Pan. But Nature has another side which experience and sin quickly discover, and it wouldn't be flippant to say the god Pan soon showed the cloven hoof.

The only objection to the religion of Nature is that somehow it always becomes unnatural. A man loves Nature in the morning for her innocence and pleasant demeanor, and then at nightfall, if he is still loving her, it is for her darkness and her cruelty. He washes at dawn in clear water like the model Stoic, yet, somehow at the dark end of the day, he is bathing in hot bull's blood as did Roman Emperor Julian the Apostate when he tried to reverse his Christian baptism.

The mere pursuit of health always leads to something unhealthy. Physical nature shouldn't be made the direct object of obedience; it must be enjoyed, not worshipped. Stars and mountains shouldn't be taken seriously. If they are, we end where the nature worship of Greco-Roman Paganism ended. Because the earth is kind, we can then imitate all her cruelties. Because sexuality is sane, we can then all go wild about sexuality. Simple optimism had reached its insane and fitting ending. The theory that everything was good had become an orgy of everything that was bad.

On the other hand, our idealistic pessimists were represented by the remaining Stoics. Marcus Aurelius and his friends had really given up on the idea of any god in the universe and looked only to the god within. They had no hope of finding any virtue in nature, and hardly any hope of any virtue in society. They didn't have enough interest in the outer world to wreck it or revolutionize it. They didn't love the city enough to set fire to it.

The Worship of a Creator

The ancient world was exactly in our present-day dilemma. The only people who really enjoyed this world were busy tearing it up, and the virtuous people didn't care enough about it to stop them. In this dilemma (the same as ours) Christianity suddenly stepped in and offered a single, remarkable answer, which the world eventually accepted as *the* answer. It was the answer then, and I think it is the answer now.

This answer was like the slash of a sword. It separated. It did not in any sentimental or emotional way unite. In short, it separated God from the cosmos. That transcendence and distinctness of God which some Christians now want to remove from Christianity was really the only reason why anyone wanted to be a Christian in the first place. It was the whole point of the Christian answer to the unhappy pessimist and the even more unhappy optimist. I will only briefly explain this metaphysical idea.

The root phrase for all Christian philosophy is this: God is a creator, just as an artist is a creator. A poet is so separate from his poem that he himself speaks of it as a little thing he has "thrown out there." Even in creating it he has thrown it away. This principle that all creation and procreation is a breaking off is at least as true and consistent throughout the cosmos as the evolutionary principle that all growth is a branching out. A woman *loses* a child even in *having* a child. All creation is separation. Birth is as somber a parting as death.

It was the main philosophical principle of Christianity that this divorce in the divine act of creating (like severing the poet from the poem or the mother from the new-born child) was the correct description of how the absolute energy made the world. According to most philosophers, God enslaved the world by making it. According to Christianity, in making it, He set it free. God had written not so much a poem, but rather a play–a play he had planned as perfect but had unavoidably been left to human actors and stage managers who had since made a great mess of it.

I will discuss the truth of this theory later. I am only going to point out here the surprising smoothness with which it solved the dilemma we have discussed in this chapter. In this way of thinking, at least a person could be both happy and angry without lowering oneself to be either a pessimist or an optimist. In this system, one could fight all the forces of life without deserting the flag of life. One could be at peace with the universe and yet be at war with the world.

St. George, who slayed a dragon according to legend, could still fight the dragon, no matter how big the monster loomed in the cosmos, even if he was bigger than the mighty cities or the everlasting hills. Even if the dragon was as big as the world itself, he could still be killed for the sake of the world. St. George didn't need to consider any obvious proportions or scale of things, but only this original secret of its creation. He can shake his sword at the dragon, even if the dragon is *everything*, even if the empty heavens over his head are only the huge arch of the dragon's open jaws.

Falling into Place

After this realization came an experience impossible to describe. It was as if I had been stumbling around since birth with two huge and unmanageable machines of different shapes that had no apparent connection to each other: the world and the Christian tradition.

First, I found this hole in the world–the fact that we must somehow find a way to love the world without trusting it. Somehow, we must love the world without being worldly. Then this feature of Christian theology stuck out to me like a hard spike: the dogmatic insistence that God was personal, and that he had made a world separate from himself.

The spike of dogma fit exactly into the hole in the world–someone had apparently meant for it to go there–and then the strangest thing began to happen. Once these two parts of the two machines came together, then, one after another, all the other parts fit and fell together with an uncanny exactness. I could hear bolt after bolt all over the machinery falling into place with a kind of click of relief. Having got one part of the machine right, all the other parts repeated that correct behavior. Instinct after instinct was answered by Christian doctrine after Christian doctrine.

To switch the metaphor, it was like I had charged into an enemy country just to take one major fortress. And when that fortress had fallen, the whole country surrendered and turned to my side. The whole land was illuminated, you could say, back to the first fields of my childhood. All those blind feelings of boyhood which, in the fourth chapter, I tried in vain to draw for you on the darkness became suddenly clear and sane.

I was right when I felt that roses were red because of some sort of choice. It was the *divine* choice. I was right when I felt that I would almost rather say grass was the wrong color than to say it always must have been that color. It truly might have been any other. My sense that happiness hung on a crazy thread of a condition really did mean something when all was said and done. It meant the whole doctrine of the Fall of man. Even those faint and shapeless monsters of ideas which I haven't been able to describe, much less defend, stepped quietly into their places like colossal statues supporting the faith.

The feeling that the cosmos wasn't vast and void, but instead small and cozy, had a fulfilled significance now, because anything that is a work of art must be small in the sight of the artist; the stars might be only tiny and dear to God, like diamonds. And my haunting instinct that somehow good wasn't simply a tool to be used, but instead a holy relic to be guarded, like the goods from Crusoe's ship—even that had been the wild whisper of something originally wise, because, according to Christianity, we really were the survivors of a wreck, the crew of a golden ship that went down before the beginning of the world. But the important thing was that it completely reversed the reason for optimism. And the instant the reversal was made, it felt like the sudden relief when a bone is put back in the socket.

I had often called myself an optimist to avoid the obvious profanity of pessimism. But all the optimism of our generation had been false and discouraging for this reason: it had always been trying to prove that we fit into the world. The Christian optimism is based on the fact that we *don't* fit into the world. I had tried to be happy by telling myself man is an animal, like any other animal that looked for its food from God. But now I really was happy because I learned that man is a monster. I had been right in feeling all things were odd, because I myself was both worse and better than everything else.

The optimist's pleasure was like prose because it lingered on the naturalness of everything; the Christian pleasure was like poetry because it lingered on the unnaturalness of everything in the light of the supernatural. The modern philosopher had told me again and again I was in the right place, and I still felt depressed even though I accepted it. But when I heard I was in the *wrong* place, my soul sang for joy like a bird in spring. It was as if that knowledge flipped a switch, turning on the lights in long-lost rooms in the dark house of my childhood. I knew now why grass had always seemed to me as odd as the green beard of a giant, and why I could feel homesick at home.

6

The Paradoxes of Christianity

The real problem with this world of ours is not that it is either reasonable or unreasonable. The most common kind of problem is that it is almost reasonable, but not quite. Life is not completely illogical, but yet it is still a trap for logicians. It looks just a little bit more mathematical and consistent than it really is. Its exactness is obvious, but its inexactness is hidden. Its wildness lies waiting.

Here is one rough example of what I mean. Let's say some mathematical alien from outer space were to examine the human body. He would immediately see the essential thing about it is that it is duplicated. One man is actually two men, the man on the right exactly resembling the man on the left. Having noted there was an arm on the right and an arm on the left, a leg on the right and a leg on the left, he might go even further and find the same number of fingers on each side, the same number of toes, twin eyes, twin nostrils, and even twin lobes of the brain. In the end, he would conclude this duplication was law. And then, when he found a heart on one side, he would deduce there was another heart on the other. And just then, when he thought he was most right, he would be wrong.

It is this subtle swerving away from accuracy by an inch that is the unsettling element in everything. It seems like a sort of secret treason in the universe. An apple or an orange is round enough to get itself called round, and yet it isn't round after all. The earth itself is shaped like an orange in order to lure some simple astronomer into calling it a globe. A blade of grass is named after the blade of a sword because it comes to a point. But it doesn't.

There is this element of the quiet and incalculable in everything. It escapes the rationalist's brain, but it never escapes until the last moment. From the grand curve of the earth, we could easily infer every inch of it was curved. It would seem rational that just as a man has a left and right brain, he should also have a left and right heart. Yet scientists are still organizing expeditions to find a man's heart, just as they organize expeditions to find the North Pole. And when they try to find it, they usually end up on the wrong side of him.

Now, to judge any given insight or idea, we should test whether it guesses these hidden abnormalities or surprises. If our alien mathematician saw the two arms and two ears, he might guess the two shoulder blades and the two halves of the brain. But if he guessed that the man's heart was in the right place, then he should be called something more than just a mathematician.

This claim is exactly what I have come to suggest about Christianity. It isn't simply that Christianity arrives at logical truths, but that when Christianity suddenly becomes illogical, it has found, so to speak, an illogical truth. It not only goes right about things, but it also goes wrong (if we can say that) exactly where things go wrong. Its plan fits with these secret abnormalities and expects the unexpected. It is simple about the simple truth, but it is stubborn about the hidden truth. It will admit that a man has two hands, but it will not admit (though all the modern thinkers howl about it) the obvious conclusion that he has two hearts. My only purpose in this chapter is to point this out, to show that whenever we feel there is something odd in Christian theology, we will usually find there is something odd in the truth.

Making a Case for the Complex

I have spoken before about a meaningless phrase that states that such and such a creed can't be believed in our time. But, of course, *anything* can be believed in *any* age. Oddly enough, however, there really is a sense in which a creed, if it is believed at all, can be believed more firmly in a complex society than in a simple one. If a man finds Christianity true in modern Birmingham, he actually has better reasons for believing than if he had found it true in ancient Mercia. As the coincidence becomes more complicated, the less it can be a coincidence. If snowflakes fell in the shape of a heart, it might be an accident. But if snowflakes fell in the exact shape of the hedge maze at Hampton Court, I think we might call it a miracle.

The Christian philosophy is exactly this same kind of miracle to me. The complexities of our modern world prove the truth of the creed better than any of the simpler faith problems of the past. It was in the cosmopolitan Notting Hill and Battersea that I began to see Christianity was true. All of this–all the complex doctrines and details–is why Christianity upsets those who admire it but don't believe in it. When someone believes in something, they are proud of its complexity, just as scientists are proud of the complexity of science. It shows how rich it is in discoveries. If it is right at all, then it could only be better to be *elaborately* right. A stick might fit a hole or a stone might fit a hollow place by chance. But a key and a lock are both complex. And if a key fits a lock, then you know it is the right key.

This complex accuracy, however, makes it very difficult to do what I now must do, to describe how I gathered this truth. It is very hard for a person to defend anything of which they are completely convinced. It is relatively easy when they are only partially convinced. They are partially convinced because they have found some sort of proof of the thing, and they can explain it. But a person isn't really convinced of a philosophic theory when they find *something* proves it. They are only really convinced when they find *everything* proves it.

The more intersecting reasons they find to prove the conviction, the more bewildered they are when asked suddenly to summarize them. Imagine if someone asked an ordinary intelligent person, on the spur of the moment, "Why do you prefer civilization over savagery?" She would look around wildly at object after object, and would only be able to answer vaguely, "Well, there's that bookcase... and the oven... and pianos... and policemen." The whole case for civilization is that the case for it is complex. Civilization has done *so many things*. This huge abundance of proof should make the woman's reply very strong, but, in reality, it makes the reply nearly impossible.

So, there is a kind of crippling helplessness that comes with complete conviction. The belief is so big that it takes a long time to get the ball rolling. And we hesitate like this, oddly enough, because we don't really care where we begin. All roads lead to Rome, which is one reason why many people never get there. On the topic of this defense of Christian belief, I admit I would just as soon begin the argument with one thing as any other. I would just as soon begin it with a turnip or a taxi. But if I am going to be careful at all about making my meaning clear, then I think it will be better to continue the last chapter's arguments, which focused on the first of these mystical coincidences, or rather confirmations.

Inconsistent Accusations

Growing up, all I heard of Christian theology turned me off from it. I was a pagan at twelve years old and a complete agnostic by sixteen. And I can't understand anyone passing the age of seventeen without having asked himself these simple questions.

I did, in fact, have a vague reverence for some cosmic deity and a large interest in the historical character of the Founder of Christianity. But I certainly thought of him as a man, although perhaps I thought he was a greater man than some of his modern critics. I read the scientific and religiously skeptical writings of my time—all of it, at least, written in English and that I could find lying around, and I read nothing else on any other kind of philosophy. The comic books which I also read were, in fact, written in the healthy and heroic tradition of Christian apologetics, but I didn't know that at the time.

I never read a single line of Christian apologetics. I read as little as I can of them now. It was actually agnostic skeptics like Huxley and Herbert Spencer and Bradlaugh who brought me back to orthodox theology. They planted in my mind my first wild doubts of doubt. Our grandmothers were quite right when they said Thomas Paine and the free thinkers can unsettle a mind. They do. They unsettle mine horribly.

The reasonable thinker made me question whether reason was of any use whatsoever. And when I had finished reading the evolutionist Herbert Spencer, I had come as far as doubting (for the first time) whether evolution had happened at all. As I laid down the last of Robert Ingersoll's atheistic lectures, King Agrippa's dreadful words to Paul crossed my mind, "Almost you persuade me to be a Christian." I was desperate.

This odd effect on me by the great agnostics—the effect of triggering doubts deeper than their own—might be illustrated in many ways. As I read and re-read all the non-Christian or anti-Christian descriptions of the faith, from Huxley to Bradlaugh, a slow and serious impression grew gradually but vividly in my mind—the impression that Christianity must be quite an extraordinary thing. Because not only (as I understood) did Christianity have the most fiery faults, but it apparently had a mystical talent for combining faults that seemed inconsistent with one another. It was attacked on all sides and for all contradictory reasons. No sooner had one rationalist shown Christianity was too far to the east than another demonstrated with equal clarity it was much too far to the west. No sooner had my anger died down at its sharp and aggressive squareness than I was riled up again to notice and attack its weak and debilitating roundness. In case any reader hasn't come across what I am describing, I will give examples as I remember them of this self-contradiction in the argument of skeptics. I will give four or five of them, but there are fifty more.

Too Optimistic and Too Pessimistic

For instance, I was very moved by the eloquent attack on Christianity that it was a thing of inhuman gloom, because I thought (and still think) sincere pessimism is the unpardonable sin. (Insincere pessimism is a social accomplishment, more pleasant than anything. And fortunately, almost all pessimism is insincere.) But if Christianity was, as these people said, a purely pessimistic thing and opposed to life, then I was thoroughly prepared to blow up St. Paul's Cathedral. But the extraordinary thing is this. They proved to me in chapter one of their atheist textbook (to my complete satisfaction) that Christianity was too pessimistic. And then, in chapter two, they began to prove it was way too optimistic.

One accusation against Christianity was that through scare tactics it kept men from seeking joy and freedom in the heart of Nature. But another accusation was that it comforted men with a fake security and laid them in a pink-and-white nursery. One great agnostic asked why Nature wasn't beautiful enough, and why it was hard to be free. The next great agnostic disagreed and stated that Christian optimism—what Huxley calls "the garment of make-believe woven by pious hands"–hid from us the fact that Nature was ugly, and that it was impossible to be free. One rationalist had hardly finished calling Christianity a nightmare before another began to call it a fool's paradise.

This confused me. The accusations seemed inconsistent. Christianity couldn't be both the black mask on a white world and also the white mask on a black world. The condition of the Christian couldn't be both so comfortable that she was a coward to cling to her faith and so uncomfortable that she was an idiot just to stand it. If it altered a person's vision, it must alter it in one way or another; it couldn't wear both black *and* rose-colored glasses.

Like all young people of that time, I rolled on my tongue the taunts that Swinburne hurled at the bleakness of the faith:

> *Thou hast conquered, O pale Galilean,*
> *The world has grown gray with Thy breath.*

But when I read the same poet's descriptions of pre-Christian paganism, I gathered that the world was, if possible, more gray before Christ breathed on it than after. The poet declared, in fact, that life itself was pitch dark, abstractly speaking. And yet, somehow, Christianity had darkened it. The very man who condemned Christianity for pessimism was a pessimist himself. I thought there must be something wrong. And for one wild moment this thought crossed my mind: maybe these people might not be the best judges of the connection between religion and happiness. By their own account, they had neither one nor the other.

I want to be clear that I didn't quickly conclude these accusations against Christianity were false or the accusers were fools. I simply inferred that Christianity must be something even weirder and more wicked than they described. A thing might possibly have two opposite vices, but that would make it a fairly peculiar thing. A man might be too fat in one place and too thin in another, but he would have an odd shape. At this point my thoughts were only on the odd shape of the Christian religion. I hadn't yet guessed the oddly shaped mind of the rationalist.

Too Violent and Too Non-Violent

Here is another example of the same kind. I felt there was a strong case against Christianity in the accusation that there is something timid, monkish, and unmanly about anything called "Christian," especially in its attitude toward resistance and fighting. The great skeptic thinkers of the nineteenth century were mostly strong and masculine. Bradlaugh, in an outgoing way, and Huxley, in a reserved way, were both unmistakably manly. In comparison, it did seem arguable that there was something weak and over-patient about Christian philosophy. The Gospel paradox about turning the other cheek, the fact that priests never fought, and a hundred other things made it plausible that Christianity was an attempt to make a man too much like a sheep.

I read this and believed it, and if I hadn't read anything different, I would have kept believing it. But I read something very different. I turned the next page in my agnostic manual, and my brain turned upside down. Now I found Christianity was to be hated not for fighting too little, but for fighting too much. Christianity, it seemed, was the mother of all wars. Christianity had flooded the world with blood. I became thoroughly angry with the Christian because he himself was never angry. And now I was told to be angry with him because his anger had been the biggest and most horrible thing in human history, as if his anger had covered the earth in blood and smoke. The people who disapproved of Christianity because of the meekness and non-resistance of the monks were the same people who also disapproved of the violence and valor of the Crusades. It was the fault of poor old Christianity (somehow or another) that both the pacifist king Edward the Confessor *didn't* fight and that the warrior king Richard the Lionheart *did*. The Quakers characterized all of Christianity in their peacefulness, and yet the massacres that cleared the way for English Quakers to move into Ireland were somehow characteristic Christian crimes.

What could it all mean? What was this Christianity that always prohibited war, yet always produced wars? What was this thing that someone could abuse first because it wouldn't fight, and then second because it was always fighting? From what puzzling world did this monstrous murder and this monstrous meekness come? The shape of Christianity grew stranger every second.

Universal Ethics versus Changing Ethics

I will give a third example. It is the strangest of all because it involves the one real objection to the faith. The one real objection to the Christian religion is simply that it is one religion. The world is a big place, full of very different kinds of people; Christianity began in Palestine, and it has practically stopped in Europe.

I was very well impressed with this argument in my youth, and I was drawn to the doctrine often preached among the humanists–I mean the doctrine that there is one huge unconscious church connecting all of humanity built on our common sense of morality. Religions, they said, divided men. But at least morals united them. A soul might seek out the strangest and most distant lands and times and still find basic ethical common sense. A soul might find the Chinese philosopher Confucius sitting under Eastern trees, and he would be writing, "Thou shalt not steal." A soul might translate the darkest hieroglyph in the most ancient desert, and the meaning when translated would be, "Little boys should tell the truth."

I believed this doctrine, that the brotherhood of all men possesses a moral sense, and I still believe it–along with other things. And I was thoroughly annoyed with Christianity for suggesting (as I thought) that entire ages and empires of men had completely missed this light of justice and reason. But then I found a shocking thing. I found that the very people who said mankind was one church all the way from Plato to Ralph Waldo Emerson were the very people who said morality had changed completely, and that what was right in one time in history was wrong in another. If I asked them, let's say, for a religious altar, I was told I didn't need one, because the brotherhood of our fellow man gave us clear prophecies and one creed in our universal customs and morals. But if I mildly pointed out that one of these universal morals was *to have an altar*, then my agnostic teachers turned right around and told me people had always been in darkness and the superstitions of savages.

I found this was their daily taunt against Christianity, saying it was the light of just one people and had left all the others to die in the dark. Their main insult to Christianity was actually their main compliment to themselves, and all their insistence on these two relative things seemed strangely unfair. When thinking of some pagan or agnostic person, we were supposed to remember all people had one religion; when thinking of some mystic or spiritualist, we were supposed to consider what absurd religions some people had. We could trust the ethics of the philosopher Epictetus because ethics had never changed. But we couldn't trust the ethics of the theologian Bossuet because ethics *had* changed. They changed in two hundred years, but not in two thousand. This started to become alarming.

It wasn't so much that Christianity looked bad enough to include any vices–the alarming thing was that any old stick seemed good enough to beat Christianity with. What, again, could this astonishing thing be like–a thing that people were so anxious to contradict, and that in doing so they didn't mind contradicting themselves? I saw the same thing everywhere I looked.

A Few More Examples of Inconsistent Accusations

I can't give much more time to this topic, but in case anyone thinks I have unfairly selected three coincidental examples, I will run briefly through a few others. So, certain skeptics wrote that the great crime of Christianity had been its attack on the family, that it had dragged women away from their homes and their children and into the loneliness and contemplation of the nunnery. But then, other skeptics (slightly more advanced) said the great crime of Christianity was that it forced the family and marriage upon us, that it doomed women to the toil of their homes and children and prohibited them from loneliness and contemplation. The accusation was reversed.

Or, again, the anti-Christians said certain phrases in the New Testament letters or even in wedding services showed disrespect to women's intellect. But I found the anti-Christians themselves disrespected women's intellect, because their great mocking remark toward the Church on the European continent was that "only women" were involved.

Or, once more, Christianity was criticized for its poor and hungry habits, for its sackcloth and dried peas. But the next minute Christianity was criticized for its excessive pomp and its ritualism, for its crystal shrines and golden robes. It was abused for being both too plain and too colored.

Again, Christianity had always been accused of restraining sexuality too much, when Bradlaugh the Malthusian, who believed the world's population would one day outgrow the food supply, discovered it didn't restrain sexuality enough.

It is often accused of being too stuffy and proper, and in the same breath of being too extravagant. Between the covers of the same atheistic pamphlet I have found the faith criticized for its division– "One thinks one thing, and the next thinks another"–and criticized also for its union– "It is difference of opinion that prevents the world from going to the dogs."

The Right Shape

I wanted to be quite fair then, and I still want to be quite fair now. I didn't conclude that the attack on Christianity was all wrong. I only concluded that if Christianity was wrong, it was, in fact, very wrong. Such opposing horrors might possibly be combined in one thing, but that thing must be very strange and isolated. There are people who are money-hoarders and also spendthrifts, but they are rare. There are people who are sensual and also disciplined, but they are rare. But if this pile of wild contradictions really existed–pacifistic and bloodthirsty, too gorgeous and too tattered, modest, yet catering preposterously to the lust of the eye, the enemy of women and their foolish refuge, a somber pessimist and a silly optimist–if this evil existed, then there was something extraordinary and unique about it.

My rationalist teachers didn't give any explanation for this exceptional corruption, because in their eyes Christianity (theoretically speaking) was only one of the ordinary myths and mistakes of mortals. They didn't give me an answer to this twisted and unnatural badness. This evil paradox rose in my mind to the stature of something supernatural. It was, in fact, almost as supernatural as the infallibility of the Pope. A significant institution that has never done anything right is just as much of a miracle as an institution that can't go wrong.

The only explanation that immediately came to mind was that Christianity didn't come from Heaven, but from Hell. Really, if Jesus of Nazareth wasn't Christ, he must have been the Antichrist. And then, in a quiet hour, a strange thought struck me like a thunderbolt. Another explanation suddenly came into my mind.

Suppose that many people had been talking about an unknown man. Suppose we were confused to hear some people say he was too tall and some say too short. Some objected to his fatness, some objected to his slimness. Some thought his complexion too dark, and some too fair. One explanation (that I have already admitted) would be that maybe he is an odd shape. But there is another explanation. Maybe he is the *right* shape. Outrageously tall men might feel he is too short. Very short men might feel he is too tall. Plump folks might consider him insufficiently filled out. Skinny folks might feel he expanded beyond the thin lines of elegance. Maybe Swedes (who have pale hair) called him a dark man, while black men considered him distinctly blonde.

To come to the point, maybe this extraordinary thing is really the ordinary thing, or at least the normal thing, the center. Maybe, after all, it is Christianity that is sane and all its critics that are insane–in various ways. I tested this theory by asking myself whether there was anything dark about my accusers that might explain their accusation. I was surprised to find this key fit a lock.

For instance, it was definitely odd that the modern world attacked Christianity both for bodily plainness and for artistic pomp. But then it was also odd–very odd–that the modern world itself combined extreme bodily luxury with an extreme absence of artistic pomp. The modern man thought Saint Thomas of Canterbury's robes too rich and his meals too poor. But, as it turns out, the modern man was actually quite unusual in history–no man before him ever ate such elaborate dinners in such ugly clothes. The modern man found the church to be too simple right where modern life is too complex; he found the church to be too gorgeous right where modern life is too dull. The man who disliked the plain fasts and feasts was wild about fancy entrées. The man who disliked religious robes wore a pair of ridiculous pants. And surely if anything was insane here it was the pants, and not the plain and simple robe. If anything was insane, it was the extravagant entrée, not the communion bread and wine.

I went over all the accusations, and I found that the key fit so far. The fact that the atheist Swinburne was irritated by the unhappiness of Christians and yet more irritated by their happiness was easily explained. It was no longer a complicated disease in Christianity, but instead a complicated disease in Swinburne. The constraints of Christians saddened him simply because he was more of a pleasure-seeker than a healthy man should be. The faith of Christians angered him because he was more pessimistic than a healthy man should be. In the same way, the Malthusians, the people who believe in strict population control, by instinct attacked Christianity, not because there is anything especially anti-Malthusian about Christianity, but because there is something a little anti-human about Malthusianism.

The Collision of Two Passions

Nevertheless, I felt it couldn't be true that Christianity was simply sensible and that it balanced in the middle. There really was an element of weight to it, and even wildness, which had justified those shallow criticisms. Christianity might be wise–I began to feel more and more that it was wise–but it wasn't wise in a simply worldly way. It didn't simply have a nice, respectable temperament. Its fierce crusaders and meek saints might balance each other, but still, the crusaders were *very* fierce and the saints were *very* meek, meek beyond anything respectable.

Now, it was right at this point of questioning that I remembered my thoughts about martyrdom and suicide. In that situation, there had been this combination of two almost insane positions which still somehow amounted to sanity. This contradiction of ferocity and meekness was exactly like that, and similarly, I found the combination to be right. This was exactly one of the paradoxes in which skeptics thought the faith wrong, but I thought it right. As wildly as Christians might love the martyr or hate suicide, they had never been as wildly passionate about these feelings as me, even long before I ever dreamed of Christianity.

Then the most difficult and interesting part of the mental process cleared, and I began to roughly trace this idea through all the huge thoughts of our theology. This is the same idea as the one I touched upon about the optimist and pessimist–the idea that we don't want a mixture or a compromise, but instead we want both things at the top of their energy. We want love and wrath burning together.

Here I will only outline this as it relates to ethics. But I don't need to remind the reader that the idea of this combination is, in fact, essential in orthodox theology, because orthodox theology has specifically insisted that Christ was not a being separate from God and man, like an elf, nor was he half human and half not, like a centaur. Instead, he was both things at once and both things completely, very man and very God. Now, let me outline this idea as I discovered it.

All sane men can see sanity is defined by some kind of equilibrium. A man may be crazy because he eats too much or crazy because he eats too little. However, some modern thinkers have proposed vague ideas of progress and evolution that attempt to destroy this balance, or what Aristotle called the "Golden Mean." They seem to suggest we should steadily starve ourselves, or instead that we should continue eating larger and larger breakfasts every morning forever. But the great, obvious truth of the Golden Mean still applies for all thinking men, and those moderns haven't upset any balance except their own.

So, if we take for granted this fact that everyone should keep some sort of balance, then the real question becomes how that balance can be kept. That was the problem Paganism tried to solve. That was the problem I think Christianity did solve and solved in a very strange way. The Paganism of Aristotle declared that virtue was found in a balance. But Christianity declared it was found in a conflict–the collision of two passions apparently inconsistent and opposite one another. Of course, they weren't *really* inconsistent, but they were in such a position that it was hard to hold them at the same time.

The Case of Courage

Let's follow for a moment the clue of martyrdom and suicide and take the case of courage. No other quality has ever confused the brains and tangled the definitions of simply rational scholars. Courage is almost a contradiction in terms. It means a strong desire to live taking the form of a readiness to die. When the gospels say, "Whoever loses their life will save it," it isn't a piece of mystic guidance for saints and heroes. It is a piece of everyday advice for sailors and mountain climbers. It could be written in an Alpine guide or a drill book.

This paradox is the whole principle of courage, even of simply worldly or savage courage. Man can only escape death by continually stepping within an inch of it. If a soldier surrounded by enemies is to fight his way out, he needs to combine a strong desire for life with a strange carelessness for death. He can't simply cling to life, because then he will be a coward and won't escape. He can't simply wait for death, because then he will be committing suicide and won't escape. He must seek after his own life in a spirit of wild indifference to it; he must desire life like water and yet drink death like wine.

I like to think that no philosopher has ever expressed this romantic riddle with enough clarity, and I certainly haven't done it. But Christianity has done more. It has marked the boundaries of it in the graves of the suicide and the hero, showing how far apart is the person who dies for the sake of living from the person who dies for the sake of dying. And this distinction has held up ever since in the mystery of knightly chivalry, in the banners that flow from European lances. Chivalry is the Christian courage, which is a disdain of death, not the Eastern courage, which is a disdain of life.

Pride and Humility

At this point I began to find this two-part passion was the Christian key to ethics in everything. Christianity made a moderation everywhere out of the crash of two powerful emotions. Take, for instance, the matter of humility, of the balance between pride and prostration, of strength and weakness. The average pagan, like the average agnostic, would simply say he is content with himself, but not arrogantly self-satisfied. He would say there are many better than him and many worse, that the rewards he has earned are limited, but he will make sure he gets them. In short, he walks with his head in the air, but not necessarily with his nose in the air.

This is a reasonable way to think, but it is open to the attack we noted against the compromise between optimism and pessimism–it is a sort of giving up. Mixing the two things makes them a watered-down version of themselves; neither has its full strength or contributes its full color. This conventional pride doesn't inspire a heart like the tongues of trumpets. You can't ride into battle with this kind of pride.

On the other hand, this mild humility of the rationalist doesn't cleanse the soul with fire and make it clear like crystal. It doesn't (like an intense and searching humility) turn a man into a little child, who can look up to the grass. It doesn't make him tilt his head up and see wonders, because Alice must become small if she is to be Alice in Wonderland.

Consequently, it loses both the poetry of pride and the poetry of humility. Christianity, in the same strange way as before, sought to save them both. Christianity separated the two ideas and then amplified them. In one way, man was to be more arrogant than he had ever been before; in another way, he was to be humbler than he had ever been before. To the extent that I am Man, I am the chief of creatures; to the extent that I am *a* man, I am the chief of sinners.

Any kind of humility that had acted like pessimism, that had taken a vague and spiteful view of a person's destiny–all of that was to go. The cries of Ecclesiastes that humanity had no superiority over the beasts, or the awful cry of Homer that man was only the saddest of all the beasts of the field–we were to hear no more of this. Man was a statue of God walking around in the garden. Man had superiority over all the beasts; man was only sad because he wasn't a beast at all, but a broken god. The Greeks had spoken of men creeping along the earth, as if clinging to it. Now Man was to walk on the earth as if to subdue it.

Christianity gave so much dignity to man that it could only be expressed with crowns that shined like the sun and fans of peacock plumage. Yet, at the same time, Christianity could view man as degradingly small—a smallness that could only be expressed in fasting and wild submission, in the gray ashes of St. Dominic and the white snows of St. Bernard. When a man stopped to think about himself, there was room enough for any amount of bleak self-rejection, of realizing the bitter truth about himself. In this place, the realistic gentleman could let himself go—as long as he let himself go at himself. This was an open playground for the happy pessimist. He could say anything against himself, as long as he didn't blaspheme the original purpose of his being. He could call himself a fool, and even a damned fool (although that is Calvinistic), but he must not say that fools aren't worth saving. He must not say that a man can be valueless.

Here, again in short, Christianity overcame the difficulty of combining raging opposites by keeping them both and keeping them both raging. The Church was positive on both points. You can hardly think too little of your *self*, but you can hardly think too much of your *soul*.

Love and Wrath

Let's take another case—the complicated question of brotherly love, which some very unloving idealists seem to think is quite easy. Love is a paradox, like humility and courage. To state it roughly, love means one of two things: forgiving unforgivable acts or caring for unlovable people. But if we asked a reasonable pagan about this subject (as we did with the case of pride), he would probably begin at the bottom of it. A reasonable pagan would say there were some people one could forgive, and some people one couldn't. A slave who stole wine could be laughed at; a slave who betrayed his owner could be killed and cursed even after he was killed. To the extent the act was forgivable, the man was also forgivable. That, again, is rational, and even refreshing. But it is watered down. It leaves no room for being horrified at injustice or for loving someone simply for being a person.

Christianity arrived as it did before. It came in surprisingly with a sword and split one thing from another. It divided the crime from the criminal. The criminal we must forgive seventy times seven. The crime we must not forgive at all. It wasn't enough that slaves who stole wine triggered partly anger and partly kindness. We must be much angrier with theft than before, and yet much more kind to thieves than before. There was room for love and wrath to run wild. Christianity had established rules and order, but the more I thought about it, the more I found the main purpose of that order was to give room for good things to run wild.

Huge and Heroic Ethics:
A Healthy Hatred of Pink

Mental and emotional freedom are not as simple as they look. In reality, they require almost as careful a balance of laws and conditions as do social and political freedom. The ordinary artistic anarchist, whose goal is to feel everything, in the end gets tangled in a paradox that prevents her from feeling anything at all. She breaks away from the limits of her home to chase poetry. But in ceasing to feel these home limits, she has ceased to feel the story of the *Odyssey*. She is free from national prejudices and she has escaped the shackles of patriotism. But being outside of patriotism, she is also outside the patriotism of *Henry V.* A literary person like this is simply outside all literature. She is more of a prisoner than any conservative. Because if there is a wall between you and the world, it doesn't make much difference whether you describe yourself as locked in or locked out.

What we want is not everything that is outside all normal feelings; we want everything that is inside all normal feelings. This is the difference between being free *from* all normal feelings and being free *of* them. I am free *from* the British government to the extent that I am not forcibly imprisoned by it. But I am by no means free *of* the British government. So, how can man be more or less free of these sharp emotions, able to swing them in a clear space without breaking anything? This was the achievement of the Christian paradox of the parallel passions. Taking for granted the primary Christian dogma of the war between Good and Evil, the revolt and ruin of the world, then optimism and pessimism, as pure poetry, could be opened like floodgates.

St. Francis, when he praised everything good, could be a louder optimist than Walt Whitman. St. Jerome, when he rejected everything evil, could paint the world blacker than the atheist Schopenhauer. Both passions were free because both were kept in their place. The optimist could pour out all the praise he wanted on the cheerful music of the soldier's march, the golden trumpets, and the purple banners in battle. But he can't call the fight needless. The pessimist might paint the sickening marches or the blood-red wounds as darkly as he wanted. But he can't call the fight hopeless.

This was the case with all other moral problems as well–with pride, with protest, and with compassion. By clarifying this main doctrine, the Church not only kept seemingly inconsistent things side by side, but, to take it even further, the Church allowed these things to break out in a sort of artistic violence that was otherwise possible only to anarchists. Meekness became more dramatic than madness. Historic Christianity rose into an exciting and strange moral turn of events–these Christian things were to virtue what the crimes of the emperor Nero were to vice. The qualities of outrage and of charity took both frightful and attractive shapes, ranging from the ferocity of the monks who whipped King Henry

The Prophet of Fleet Street

Chesterton often speaks with surprising confidence, but it's difficult to dismiss his assertiveness when so many of his predictions have proven accurate, particularly in his analysis of revolution. For example, he correctly foresaw both the rise and fall of communism in Russia, and he even anticipated the emergence of a rigid bureaucracy and the eventual liberation of small nations from its grip. More than a decade before the Russian revolution began, Chesterton wrote, "A country like Russia has far more inherent capacity for producing revolution than any country of the type of England or America." Other Chesterton "prophecies" include the outbreak of World War II, specifically predicting it would "probably start on the Polish border"; that the airplane would mean war against not just soldiers but also civilians; that with the rapid rise of technology, "civilization has run on ahead of the soul of man and is producing faster than he can think and give thanks"; that there would be an assault on morality, especially sexual morality, claiming we would "exalt lust and forbid fertility"; and that the "old parental authority" would be replaced "not by liberty or even license, but by the far more sweeping and destructive authority of the State."

II like a dog for murdering the Archbishop of Canterbury, to the awe-inspiring compassion of St. Catherine, who accompanied a criminal to the chopping block, caught his bloody head, and kissed it. Poetry can be acted as well as written.

This huge and heroic approach to ethics has completely vanished within supernatural religion. Those people, being humble, could flaunt themselves. But we are too proud to be prominent. Our ethics teachers write reasonably for prison reform, but we aren't likely to see any famous philanthropists like Mr. Cadbury go into prison and embrace a strangled corpse before it is disposed. They write mildly against the power of millionaires, but we aren't likely to see the oil tycoon Mr. Rockefeller, or any other modern tyrant, publicly whipped in Westminster Abbey.

So, the parallel accusations of the secularists, although they shed nothing but darkness and confusion on themselves, shed a real light on the Christian faith. It is true that historically the Church has both encouraged abstinence and encouraged the growth of the family. If I can put it this way, it has been both fiercely *for* having children and fiercely for *not* having children. It has kept them side by side like two strong colors, red and white, like the red and white of the English flag.

Christianity has always had a healthy hatred of pink. It hates that combination of two colors that is easy and weak and is so often used by philosophers. It hates that evolution of black into white that is really only a dirty gray. In fact, the Church's whole stance on virginity might be summed up by the statement that white is a color, not simply the absence of a color. All I am saying here is that the goal of Christianity in most of these cases was to keep two colors coexistent but pure.

This is also true, of course, of the contradictory accusations of the anti-Christians about submission and slaughter. It is true that the Church told some men to fight and others not to fight. And it is true that those who fought struck like thunderbolts, and those who didn't were as submissive as statues. All of this means the Church simply preferred to use its fighters as well as its pacifists.

There must be *some* good in the life of war, because so many good men have enjoyed being soldiers. And there must be *some* good in the idea of non-resistance, because so many good men seem to enjoy being Quakers. All the Church did (in this case) was to prevent either of these good things from driving out the other. They existed side by side. The pacifists, being as uneasy toward war as the monks, simply became monks, and the Quakers became a denomination instead of a cult. Monks said all that pacifists say; they cried out with rational grievances about the cruelty of battles and the uselessness of revenge. But the pacifists aren't quite right enough to run the whole world. And throughout the history of our faith, they weren't allowed to run it. The world didn't lose the last charge of Sir James Douglas or the war banner of Joan of Arc. And at times this pure gentleness and this pure ferocity have met and joined; the paradox of all the prophets was fulfilled, and, in the soul of St. Louis, king of France, ferocity met gentleness, and the lion lay down with the lamb.

Remember, however, that this scripture is often misinterpreted. It is constantly said, especially due to our meeker Tolstoyan tendencies, that when the lion lies down with the lamb, the lion becomes lamb-like. But that is a brutal, imperialistic conquering on the part of the lamb. That is simply the lamb absorbing the lion instead of the lion eating the lamb. The real question is this. Can the lion lie down with the lamb and still keep his royal ferocity? *That* is the problem the Church attempted to answer. *That* is the miracle she achieved.

The Discovery of the New Balance

This is what I was referring to when I spoke of Christianity guessing the hidden eccentricities of life. It means knowing a man's heart is to the left and not in the middle. It means knowing not only that the earth is round, but also knowing exactly where it is flat. Christian doctrine uncovered the strange things of life. It not only discovered the law, but it predicted the odd exceptions to the law.

Those who say Christianity discovered mercy are minimizing it; anyone could discover mercy. In fact, everyone did. But to discover a plan for being both merciful *and* severe—that was a prediction of a strange human need. Anyone might say we shouldn't be either extremely miserable or extremely happy. But to find out how extremely miserable a person may be without making it impossible to be extremely happy—that was a discovery in psychology. Anyone might say, "You shouldn't strut high, nor should you stoop low," and this would have put boundaries on behavior. But to say, "*Here* you can strut high and *there* you can stoop low"—now that is an emancipation.

This was the big fact about Christian ethics: the discovery of the new balance. Paganism had been like a pillar of marble. It stood upright because it was proportioned equally on both sides. Christianity was like a huge and jagged and romantic rock. It sways on its pedestal at the slightest touch, and yet, because its exaggerated outgrowths exactly balance each other, it is enthroned there for a thousand years. In a Gothic cathedral, the columns were all different, but they were all necessary. Every supporting pillar seemed accidental and fantastic. Likewise, within Christendom, apparent accidents balanced each other.

Archbishop Thomas Becket wore a shirt of goat hair under his crimson and gold garments to torment his body, and there is much to be said for that combination of clothing–Becket benefited from the hair shirt, and the people in the street benefited from the crimson and gold. It is at least better than the ways of the modern millionaire. He wears the black and dull clothing for others and keeps the gold next to his heart.

The balance wasn't always in one man's body as it was in Becket's. The balance was often spread over the whole body of Christendom. Because a man prayed and fasted in the North, flowers could be flung at festivals in the Southern cities. And because fanatics only drank water on the sands of Syria, men could still drink cider in the orchards of England. This is what makes Christianity both much more confusing and much more interesting than the Pagan empire. It is the same reason why Amiens Cathedral in France isn't *better* than the Greek Parthenon, just more interesting.

If anyone wants a modern example of this, then let's consider the curious fact that, under Christianity, Europe (while remaining a unit) has broken up into individual nations. Patriotism is a perfect example of this purposeful balancing of one emphasis against another emphasis. The instinct of the Pagan empire would have said, "You will all be Roman citizens, and become alike. Let the German become less slow and reverent. Let the Frenchman become less experimental and swift." But the instinct of Christian Europe says, "Let the

German remain slow and reverent, so that the Frenchman can more safely be experimental and swift. We will counterbalance these excesses. The absurdity called Germany will correct the insanity called France."

The Thrilling Romance of Orthodoxy

Lastly and most importantly, it is specifically this that explains what is so inexplicable to all the modern critics of the history of Christianity, and I mean the monstrous wars over small points of theology, the earthquakes of emotion over a gesture or a word. After all, it was only a matter of an inch. But an inch is everything when you are balancing.

The Church couldn't afford to swerve a hair's breadth on some things if she was to continue her awesome and daring experiment of balancing irregular things. If you let one idea become less powerful, then some other idea would become too powerful. It wasn't a flock of sheep the Christian shepherd was leading, but instead a herd of bulls and tigers, of frightful ideals and devouring doctrines, each one of them strong enough to turn into a false religion and lay waste to the world. Remember that the Church came specifically for dangerous ideas; she was a lion tamer. The idea of birth through a Holy Spirit, of the death of a divine being, of the forgiveness of sins, or the fulfillment of prophecies–anyone can see that all of these ideas need only a touch to turn them into something blasphemous or ferocious. The smallest link in the chain was forgotten by the Christian builders of the Mediterranean and the pessimism of their ancestors, that ferocious lion, burst loose in the forgotten forests of the north.

I will wait to speak about these matters of theological balances. But here it is enough to notice that if some small mistake were made in doctrine, huge blunders might be made in human happiness. A sentence phrased wrong about the nature of symbolism would have broken all the best statues in Europe. A wrong definition might stop all the dances, might wither all the Christmas trees, or break all the Easter eggs. Doctrines had to be defined within strict limits even just for man to enjoy simple human freedoms. The Church had to be careful, if only so the world could be careless.

This is the thrilling romance of Orthodoxy. People have gotten into the idiotic habit of calling orthodoxy heavy, humdrum, and safe. There was never anything so dangerous or so exciting as orthodoxy. It was sanity, and to be sane is more dramatic than to be insane. It was the balance of a charioteer behind wildly rushing horses, seeming to sway back and forth, yet in every way having the grace of a statue and accuracy of arithmetic. In its early days, the Church went along fierce and fast with any warhorse, yet it is utterly wrong and unhistorical to say she simply went wild along the path of one idea, like some vulgar extremism. She swerved to the left and right so accurately as to avoid enormous obstacles. On one hand she steered clear of the huge bulk of Arianism, which denied the divinity of Christ, which tried to make Christianity too worldly with the help of all the worldly powers. Next, she was swerving to avoid oriental influences, which would have made it too unworldly.

The orthodox Church never took the safe road or accepted the status quo. The orthodox Church was never respectable. It would have been easier to accept the earthly power of the Arians. It would have been easier, in the Calvinistic seventeenth century, to fall into the bottomless pit of predestination. It is easy to be a madman. And it is easy to be a heretic. It is always easy to let the generation have its head; the difficult thing is to keep your own. It is always easy to be a modernist, just as it is easy to be a snob.

To have fallen into any one of those open traps of mistakes and extremism which craze after craze and group after group set along the path of Christianity throughout history—that really would have been simple. It is always easy to fall; there are infinite angles at which a person falls, and only one at which they stand. To have fallen into any one of the fads, from Gnosticism to Christian Science, really would have been obvious and safe. But to have avoided them all has been one whirling adventure. And as I see it, the heavenly chariot continues to fly thundering through the ages, the dull heresies lying limp on the floor, the wild truth reeling but upright.

7

The Eternal Revolution

To this point, I have proposed these ideas. First, that some faith in our life is required simply to improve it. Second, that some dissatisfaction with things as they are is necessary simply to be satisfied. And third, to have this necessary contentment and necessary discontentment, it isn't sufficient to have the more obvious balance of the Stoics. Because simply giving up has neither the gigantic cheerfulness of pleasure nor the imposing intolerance of pain. It is important not to follow the advice of simply "grin and bear it," because if you simply bear it, you do not grin.

Statues of Greek heroes don't grin, but the gargoyles that sit atop Gothic cathedrals do, because they are Christian. And when a Christian is pleased, she is, as in the case of the gargoyle, terrifyingly pleased–her pleasure is terrifying. Christ prophesied all of Gothic architecture in that moment when the nervous and respectable citizens of Jerusalem objected to those who loudly praised him in the streets. He said, "If they keep silent, the very stones will cry out."

Inspired by his spirit, the Gothic cathedrals arose like a clamorous chorus, crowded with shouting faces and open mouths. The prophecy has fulfilled itself. The very stones cry out.

Competing Principles of Progress

If we assume what I have said so far to be true, if only for the sake of argument, then we can continue where we left off with the thought of the natural man. The obvious next question is this: some satisfaction is needed in order to make things better–but what do we mean by making things better?

Most modern arguments on this topic are simply circular (that circle which we have already made the symbol for madness and simple rationalism). They say evolution is only good if it produces good; they say good is only good if it helps evolution. The elephant stands on the turtle, and the turtle stands on the elephant.

Obviously, it won't work to form our ideas from some principle found in nature, for the simple reason that (except for some human or divine theory *about* nature) there is no principle in nature. For example, some modern opponents of democracy will sincerely tell you there is no equality in nature. He is right, but he doesn't see the logical next step. There is no equality in nature, but there is no inequality, either. Inequality, just as much as equality, implies some sort of standard of value. To project aristocracy onto the anarchy of animals is just as emotional and illogical as to project democracy onto it. Both aristocracy and democracy are human ideas–one of them states that all men are valuable, the other that some men are more valuable than others.

Nature, however, doesn't say that cats are more valuable than mice. Nature has no comment on the subject. She doesn't even say the cat is to be envied or the mouse is to be pitied. We consider the cat superior because we have (or at least most of us have) a particular philosophy to the effect that life is better than death. But if the mouse were a German pessimist mouse, he might not think the cat had beaten him at all. He might think he had beaten the cat by getting to the grave first. Or he might feel that he had actually inflicted a terrible punishment on the cat by keeping him alive. Just as a germ might feel proud of spreading a disease, the pessimistic mouse might rejoice to think he was continuing in the cat the torture of conscious existence. It all depends on the philosophy of the mouse.

You can't say there is victory or superiority in nature unless you have some doctrine about what things are superior. You can't say the cat scores unless there is a system of scoring. You can't say the cat gets the best of it unless there is some best to be got. We can't, then, get the principle itself from nature, and as we are creating a first and natural theory, we will leave out (for now) the idea of getting it from God. We must have our own theories.

The attempts of most modern thinkers to express these theories are highly vague. Some of their arguments rely simply on the clock. They talk as if the simple passing of time brings superiority. I have heard people of the utmost mental caliber carelessly say that "human morality is never up-to-date." But how can anything be up-to-date? A date has no character. How can someone say that Christmas parties aren't suitable for the twenty-fifth of a month? What the writer meant, of course, was that the majority of humans who have ever lived are behind his favorite minority.

Other vague moderns take refuge in physical metaphors. In fact, this is the most glaring sign of a vague modern person. They don't dare to clearly define their doctrine of what is good. Instead, they use physical figures of speech without restraint or shame, and, worst of all, they seem to think these poor analogies are exquisitely spiritual and much better than the old ideas of morality. So, they think it is intelligent to talk about things being "high." It is at least the opposite of intelligent. "Tommy was a good boy" is a pure philosophical statement, worthy of Plato or Aquinas. "Tommy lived the

---

◎ Genius on Genius ◎

When tasked with writing a book on St. Thomas Aquinas, one of the deepest and most rigorous thinkers to ever live, Chesterton took a unique approach. Rather than immersing himself in an exhaustive study, he instructed his secretary to fetch a stack of books on St. Thomas from the library. Opening the topmost book, he flipped through its pages, promptly closed it, then proceeded to dictate what Etienne Gilson called "without possible comparison, the best book ever written on St. Thomas." Gilson, a renowned historian and philosopher in his own right, said, "Nothing short of genius can account for such an achievement. Everybody will no doubt admit that it is a 'clever' book, but the few readers who have spent twenty or thirty years in studying St. Thomas. . . cannot fail to perceive that the so-called 'wit' of Chesterton has put their scholarship to shame. He has guessed all that which we had tried to demonstrate, and he has said all that which they were more or less clumsily attempting to express in academic formulas. Chesterton was one of the deepest thinkers who ever existed."

---

higher life" is a repulsive metaphor from a steeple or a weath-ervane.

Speaking of vague modern metaphors, this is almost the whole weakness of Nietzsche, who some are saying is a bold and strong thinker. No one could deny he was a poetic and evocative thinker, but he was really the opposite of strong, and he wasn't bold at all. He never put his ideas in simple words as did the hard, fearless people of thought like Aristotle, John Calvin, and even Karl Marx. Nietzsche always escaped a question by using a physical metaphor, like a cheery minor poet. He said things were "beyond good and evil" because he didn't have the courage to say they were "more good than good and evil," or, "more evil than good and evil." If he had examined his own thoughts without using metaphors, he would have seen they made no sense. When he describes the perfect man, he doesn't dare to say, "the purer man," or "the happier man," or "the sadder man," because all of these are actual ideas, and ideas are dangerous. He says, "the upper man," or "over man"–these are physical metaphors used for acrobats or mountain climbers. Nietzsche truly is a very timid thinker. He doesn't really know at all what sort of man he wants evolution to produce. And if he doesn't know, then surely the ordinary evolutionists, who talk about things being "higher," don't know either.

Then again, some are content to sit and do nothing. Nature is going to do something someday–nobody knows what, and nobody knows when. We have no reason for doing anything, and no reason for not doing anything. If anything happens, then it must be right. If anything is kept from happening, it must be wrong.

And again, others try to guess what nature is up to by doing something, by doing anything. Because humans might possibly grow wings, they decide to cut off their legs. But nature may be trying to make them centipedes for all they know.

Lastly, there is a fourth group of people who take whatever it is they happen to want and say that *that* is the ultimate goal of evolution. And this group is the only reasonable one. This is the only really healthy way to view evolution: to work for what you want, and to call that evolution. The only comprehensible approach to progress and advancement would be to have a clear vision, and then work to make everything like that vision.

To put it differently, the essence of the idea is that what we have around us is simply the procedures and the plan for something we must create. This isn't a world, but instead the material for a world. God hasn't given us so much the colors of a complete picture so much as he has given us the colors of a paint palette. But he has also given us a subject, a model, a firm vision. We must be clear about what we want to paint.

A Firm and Familiar Goal

This adds the next principle to the list of principles already discussed. We have said we must be passionate about this world even in order to change it. Now we should add that we must be passionate about another world (real or imaginary) in order to have something to change it into.

We don't need to debate about the simple words of evolution or progress. Personally, I like to call it reform, because reform implies a form. It implies we are trying to shape the world into a particular image, to make it something we already see in our minds. Evolution is a metaphor for a simple automatic unrolling. Progress is a metaphor for simply walking along a road, and more than likely the wrong road. But reform is a metaphor used by reasonable and determined people. It means we see something out of shape, we are determined to get it into shape, and that we also know what shape to get it into.

Now, this is where the huge mistake of our time comes in and causes everything to collapse. We have mixed up two different things, two opposite things. Progress *should* mean we are always changing the world to make it more like the vision. Progress *does* mean (in today's world) that we are always changing the vision, instead. It *should* mean we are slowly but surely bringing justice and mercy to the world. It *does* mean we are very quick to doubt whether we really do want justice and mercy, as does any wild page from a Prussian philosopher. Progress *should* mean we are always walking toward the New Jerusalem. It *does* mean the New Jerusalem is always walking away from us. We aren't changing the real to fit the ideal. Instead, we change the ideal because it is easier.

Silly examples are always simpler. Let's say a man wanted a particular kind of world–let's say, a blue world. He wouldn't have any reason to complain about the insignificance of the task or the time it took him to accomplish it. He might work hard at the transformation for a long time. He could work until everything was blue in every way. He could have heroic adventures, like putting the last touches on a blue tiger. He could have fairy dreams; the dawn of a blue moon. But if he worked hard, that high-minded reformer would certainly (from his own point of view) leave the world better and bluer than he found it. If he changed a blade of grass to his favorite color every day, his work would progress slowly. But, if he changed his favorite color every day, his work wouldn't progress at all. If he read a fresh philosopher and then began to paint everything red or yellow, his work would be wasted. There would be nothing to show except a few blue tigers walking around, samples of his early bad approach.

This is exactly the attitude of the average modern thinker. People will say this is a ridiculous example, as I have already admitted. But it is literally what has taken place recently. The great, serious changes in our political landscape all happened in the early nineteenth century, not the later. They happened in the clear-cut period when people believed firmly in Toryism, in Protestantism, in Calvinism, in reform, and not unfrequently in revolution. Whatever thing each person believed in, they hammered at it steadily, without hesitation. There was a time when the Church of England might have fallen, and the House of Lords almost fell. This was because radicals were wise enough to be constant and consistent; it was because radicals were wise enough to be conservative. But in the current climate there isn't enough time and tradition in radicalism to pull anything down.

There is quite a bit of truth in the conservative politician Lord Hugh Cecil's suggestion (made in an excellent speech) that the age of change is over, and that our age is one of conservation and rest. But it would probably pain Lord Hugh Cecil if he realized what is certainly true, that our age is only one of conservation because it is an age of complete unbelief.

If you want institutions to remain the same, then let beliefs fade fast and often. The more the life of the mind is unsettled, the more the machinery of earth will be left alone. The net result of all our current political movements–Collectivism, Tolstoyanism, Neo-Feudalism, Communism, Anarchy, Scientific Bureaucracy–the plain product of all of them is that the Monarchy and the House of Lords remain unchanged. The net result of all the new religions will be that the Church of England won't (for Heaven knows how long) be disestablished. It was Karl Marx, Nietzsche, Tolstoy, Cunninghame Grahame, Bernard Shaw and Auberon Herbert who between them, with gigantic and straining backs, held up the throne of the Archbishop of Canterbury.

We can make the general statement that free thought is the best way to protect against freedom. If managed in a modern way, the emancipation of the slave's mind is the best way to prevent the emancipation of the slave. Teach him to worry about whether he wants to be free, and he won't free himself.

We Did Nazi That Coming

While many turned a blind eye to the rise of communism in early 20th-century Europe, Chesterton emerged as an early voice warning against the ominous ascent of Nazi Germany. As far back as 1933, he anticipated the looming specter of war. By 1934, he had condemned the violent tactics of Hitler, stating we should "feel about Hitler as men felt about Herod." And by 1935, he articulated a scathing critique of the Nazi regime, writing, "Hitler's way of defending the independence of the family is to make every family dependent on him and his semi-Socialist State; and to preserve the authority of parents by authoritatively telling all the parents what to do... In other words, he appears to interfere with family life more even than the Bolshevists do; and to do it in the name of the sacredness of the family." As communism cast its shadow over Europe, Chesterton's foresight predicted this perilous path to war.

Again, people may say this example is isolated or extreme. But, again, it is literally true of the people in the streets around us. It is true that the human slave, being reduced to a barbarian, will probably have either a human passion for loyalty or a human passion for liberty. But the man we see every day–the worker in the factory or the little clerk in the office–she is too mentally worried to believe in freedom. She is kept quiet by revolutionary literature. She is kept calm and in her place by a constant stream of wild philosophies. She is a Marxian one day, a Nietzscheite the next day, and a slave every day. The only thing that remains after all the philosophies is the factory. The only person who benefits from all the philosophies is the boss. It would be worth his while to ensure his business slaves are supplied with skeptical literature. All modern books are on his side.

As long as the vision of Heaven is always changing, the vision of Earth will stay exactly the same. No ideal will stick around long enough to be achieved, or even partly achieved. The modern young man will never change his environment, because he will always change his mind.

So, this is the first requirement for the ideal our progress is directed toward: it must be firm. Painters often make lots of rapid sketches of a model. It wouldn't matter if they tore up twenty sketches, but it would matter if they looked up twenty times and each time saw a new person sitting patiently for their portrait. Likewise, it doesn't matter (relatively speaking) how often humanity fails to reach its goal, because then all of its old failures are fruitful. But it matters very much how often humanity changes its goal, because then all of its old failures are fruitless.

The question, then, becomes this: how can we keep the artist dissatisfied with his paintings while preventing him from being dissatisfied with his art? How can we make a man always dissatisfied with his work, yet always satisfied with working? How can we make sure the painter will throw the portrait out the window instead of doing the more natural and human thing of throwing the model out the window?

A strict rule isn't only necessary for ruling; it is also necessary for rebelling. A firm and familiar standard is necessary for any sort of revolution. New ideas will sometimes move people to act slowly, but people will only act quickly upon old ideas. If I simply float or fade or evolve, I may head toward something chaotic. But if I want to riot, it must be for something respectable.

This is the major weakness of certain ideas of progress and moral evolution. They suggest there has been a slow movement over time toward right morality, with an unnoticeable ethical change in every year or even at every moment. There is only one great disadvantage in this theory. It talks of a slow movement toward justice, but it doesn't allow for a quick movement. No one is allowed to jump up and declare a certain situation to be inherently intolerable.

To make things clear, it is better to use a specific example. Certain idealistic vegetarians say the time has come for eating no meat, which implies they think that at one time it was right to eat meat. And they suggest (in words that could be quoted) that someday it may be wrong to eat milk and eggs. I am not here to argue about justice for animals. I only say that justice, whatever it is, should be swift justice. If an animal is wronged, we should be able to rush to its rescue. But how can we rush if we are, let's say, ahead of our time? How can we rush to catch a train which may not arrive for a few hundred years? How can I criticize a man for skinning a cat if he is only committing a wrong that I will one day match by drinking a glass of milk? A lovely and insane group of Russians used to run around letting all the cattle out of all the carts. But how can I muster up the courage to free the horse from my own carriage when I don't know whether my evolutionary watch is fast or slow?

Let's say I tell a sweatshop owner, "Slavery was appropriate for only one stage of evolution." And let's say he answers, "And sweatshops are appropriate for this stage of evolution." How can I answer if there is no eternally consistent test? If sweatshops can be behind the curve of current morality, then why shouldn't philanthropists be in front of it? What on earth is the current morality except its literal meaning–the morality that is always flowing away?

So, a firm goal is just as necessary for those who want change as for those who want everything the same; a firm goal is necessary no matter if we want the king's orders to be swiftly executed or if we just want the king to be swiftly executed. The guillotine has many flaws, but to give it credit, there is nothing evolutionary about it. The most popular question of the evolutionists is best answered by this instrument of execution. The Evolutionist asks, "Where do you draw the line?" The Revolutionist answers, "I draw it *here*: right between your head and your body."

At any given moment, there must be an abstract right and wrong before any blow can be struck; there must be something eternal and permanent before anything sudden. So, for all possible human purposes, for changing things or for keeping things as they are, for perpetuating a system forever as China has or for changing it every month as in the early French Revolution, it is equally important that the goal should be a firm goal. This is our first requirement.

At this point, I felt again that something else was trying to chime in, as a man hears a church bell above the sounds of the street. Something seemed to be saying,

My *ideal, at least, is firm, because it was firm before the foundation of the world. My vision of perfection certainly can't be altered, because it is called Eden. You can change the place you are walking toward, but you can't change the place you came from.*

For the orthodox, there is always a cause for revolution. In the hearts of men, God has been placed under the feet of Satan. In the upper world, Hell once rebelled against Heaven. But in this world, Heaven is rebelling against Hell. For the orthodox, there can always be a revolution, because a revolution is a restoration. At any moment you could strike a blow in the name of perfection, a strike like no one has seen since Adam.

No unchanging tradition, no changing evolution can make that original good anything but good. Man may have had concubines for as long as cows have had horns, but they still are not a part of him if they are sinful. Men may have been under oppression ever since fish were under water, but they still shouldn't be, if oppression is sinful. The chain may seem as natural to the slave as feathers to a bird, and paint may be as comfortable to the prostitute as a burrow to a fox, but they still are not natural, if they are sinful.

I raise my prehistoric legend against all your history. This vision is not simply a fixture. It is a fact.

A Complex Goal

I paused here to note this new coincidence of Christianity, but I soon passed on. I passed on to the next necessary step of anything to do with progress. Some people (as we have said) seem to believe in an automatic and impersonal progress in things. But it is clear that we aren't encouraging any sort of political action by saying progress is natural and inevitable. Inevitable progress isn't a reason for action, but rather a reason for laziness. If we are bound to improve, we don't need to try to improve. The utter idea of progress is the best reason of all for not trying to bring about change.

But I don't mean to draw attention to any of these obvious points. The only noteworthy point to make here is this: if we claim improvement is natural, then it must also be fairly simple. We can imagine the world blindly working toward one achievement, but not really toward any particular arrangement of a large number of things. Let's go back to our original metaphor. Nature by herself might be growing more blue. This is a process so simple that it could possibly be impersonal and mindless. But Nature can't be creating a careful picture made of many chosen colors unless Nature is personal and intelligent.

If the end of the world were complete darkness or complete light, then it might come about as slowly and inevitably as dusk or dawn. But if the end of the world is meant to be a piece of elaborate blending of light and dark, then there must be a design in it, either human or divine. The world, simply by the passage of time, might grow black like an old picture or white like an old coat. But if it is turned into a particular piece of black and white art—then there is an artist.

If the distinction between the two isn't obvious, I will give an ordinary example. We hear all the time about a particularly massive idea from the modern humanitarians. (I use the word humanitarian in the usual sense, meaning someone who defends the rights of all creatures at the expense of humanity.) They suggest that through the ages humans have been growing more and more humane, and that one after another, groups of beings–slaves, children, women, cows, or what not–have gradually accepted mercy and justice.

They say we once thought it was right to eat people (which we didn't). But I am not concerned here with their history (which is extremely unhistorical). In truth, cannibalism is certainly a product of a culture in decline, not of a primitive culture that has never risen. It is much more likely that modern men will eat human flesh to impress each other than a primitive man ever ate it out of ignorance.

I am only tracing here the outlines of their argument, which claims man has grown more and more lenient, first to citizens, then to slaves, then to animals, and then (probably) to plants. I think it is wrong to sit on a man. Soon I will think it is wrong to sit on a horse. Eventually (I guess) I will think it is wrong to sit on a chair. That is the direction of the argument. And we can say about this argument that it can be spoken of in terms of evolution or inevitable progress. We feel that a perpetual tendency to touch fewer and fewer things might simply be brute and unconscious, like the tendency of a species to produce fewer and fewer children.

This mindless drifting might really be evolutionary because it is really stupid. The evolutionary theory of Darwinism can be used to support two insane kinds of moralities, but it can't be used to support a single sane one. Both the friendship and competition of all living creatures can be used as a reason for insane cruelty or insane affection, but not as a reason for a healthy love of animals. On an evolutionary basis, you may be inhumane or you may be insanely humane, but you can't be human.

The idea that you and a tiger are one may be a reason for being kind to a tiger. Or it may be a reason for being as cruel as the tiger. It is one thing to train the tiger to imitate you, it is another thing to imitate the tiger. But in neither case does evolution tell you how to treat a tiger reasonably. It doesn't tell you to admire her stripes while avoiding her claws.

If you want to treat a tiger reasonably, you must go back to the garden of Eden. I am here to stubbornly remind us again and again that only the supernatural has taken a sane view of Nature. The essence of all pantheism, evolutionism, and modern progressive spirituality is that Nature is our mother. Unfortunately, if you consider Nature your mother, then you find she is a stepmother.

The main point of Christianity was this: Nature is not our mother. Nature is our sister. We can be proud of her beauty, since we have the same father, but she has no authority over us. We must admire, but not imitate.

This gives a touch of lightness and almost silliness to the pleasure the earth gives to Christians. Nature was a somber mother to the worshipers of Isis and Cybele, the mother goddesses of Egyptian and Phrygian mythology. Nature was a somber mother to Wordsworth and Emerson, the transcendentalist writers. But Nature is not a somber mother to Francis of Assisi or to George Herbert. To St. Francis, Nature is a sister, and even a younger sister–a little, dancing sister that should be laughed at as well as loved.

This, however, is hardly our main point right now. I wrote it only to show how constantly and even accidentally the Christian key would fit the smallest locks. Our main point is that if there actually is a trend of impersonal, mindless improvement in Nature, then it must presumably be a simple trend toward some simple achievement.

It is possible to imagine that some automatic tendency in biology might work to give us longer and longer noses. But the question is, do we want to have longer and longer noses? I like to think we don't. I believe most of us want to say to our noses, "this far, and no farther, and here shall your proud point stop." We require our nose to be long enough to ensure an interesting face, but we can't imagine a simple biological trend that produces interesting faces, because an interesting face requires a particular arrangement of eyes, nose, and mouth all in a very complex relation to each other. Proportions can't be without purpose. They are either an accident or a design.

It is the same with the ideal of human morality and its relation to the humanitarians and the anti-humanitarians. It seems we are trending more and more toward keeping our hands off of things–not to ride horses, and not to pick flowers. We might eventually be kept from disturbing a someone's brain with an argument, or from disturbing the sleep of birds by even coughing. It seems the ultimate model of human perfection would be a person sitting quite still, not daring to move for fear of disturbing a fly, nor daring to eat for fear of inconveniencing a germ. And it is possible that we could unconsciously arrive at a basic achievement like this. But do we want our achievements to be this basic?

On the other hand, we might unconsciously evolve along the Nietzschean line of progress–superman crushing superman in one huge tower of tyrants until the universe is smashed up just for fun. But do we want the universe to be smashed up for fun? Isn't it quite clear that what we really hope for is one particular management and balance of these two things–a certain amount of respect and restraint, a certain amount of energy and control?

If our life is ever going to be as beautiful as a fairy tale, then we will have to remember all the beauty of the fairy tale lies in this: the prince has a wonder that stops just short of fear. If he is afraid of the giant, then that is the end of him. But, also, if he is not astonished by the giant, then that is the end of the fairy tale. The whole thing depends on him being both humble enough to marvel and haughty enough to defy. Likewise, our attitude toward the giant of the world can't simply be increasing sensitivity or increasing disrespect. It must be one particular combination of the two—a proportion that is exactly right. We must have enough reverence for everything outside us to make us walk fearfully on the grass. But we must also have enough disdain for everything outside us to make us, on occasion, spit at the stars.

And these two things (if we want to lead good and happy lives) must be combined in one particular combination, not just in *any* combination. The perfect happiness of humanity on Earth (if it ever comes) won't be a simple and solid thing, like the satisfaction we observe from animals. It will be an exact and dangerous balance, like the balance of an exciting romance. Man must have just enough faith in himself to have adventures, and just enough doubt of himself to enjoy them.

This, then, is our second requirement for the ideal of progress. First, it must be firm and fixed. Second, it must be complex, made up of various parts. It can't be (if it is to satisfy our souls) simply the victory of some one thing swallowing up everything else—love or pride or peace or adventure. It must be a specific picture made up of these elements in their best relation to one another.

I am not trying to confirm or deny here that this good culmination of things may be reserved for the human race. I only point out that if this complex happiness is fixed for us, then it must be fixed by some mind, because only a mind can exactly balance the proportions of a complex happiness. If the beautification of the world is a simple work of nature, then it could be as simple as the freezing of the world or the burning up of the world. But if the beautification of the world is not a work of nature and is instead a work of art, then it involves an artist.

And here, again, my contemplation was interrupted by the ancient voice which said,

I could have told you all of this long ago. If there is any positive progress, then it can only be my kind of progress, the progress toward a complete city of dominating virtues where righteousness and peace are made to kiss. An impersonal force might be leading you to a wilderness of perfect flatness or a peak of perfect height. But only a personal God could possibly lead you (if you actually are being led) to a city with fair streets and perfectly proportioned architecture, a city in which each of you can contribute exactly the right amount of your own color to the many-colored coat of Joseph.

An Eternal Revolution

So, Christianity had twice come in with the exact answer I needed. I said, "The ideal must be fixed," and the Church answered, "Mine is literally fixed, because it existed before anything else." Second, I said, "It must be artistically combined, like a picture," and the Church answered, "Mine is quite literally a picture, because I know who painted it."

Then I went on to the third thing, which seemed to me to be needed for a Utopia or goal of progress. And of all three, it is infinitely the hardest to express. Maybe I can put it this way: we need to be watchful even in Utopia, to avoid falling from Utopia as we fell from Eden.

We have stated that one reason people give for being a progressive is that things tend to develop better when left unattended. But the only real reason for being a progressive is that things tend to develop worse when left unattended. The natural spoiling of things is not only the best argument for being progressive, but it is also the only argument against being conservative. The conservative theory really would be tremendously extensive and indisputable if it weren't for just this one fact. All conservatism is based upon the idea that if you leave things alone, they stay as they are. But they don't. If you leave a thing alone, you leave it to a flood of change. If you leave a white post alone, it will soon be a black post. If you especially want it to be white, then you should always be painting it again. In other words, you must always be having a revolution. In short, if you want the *old* white post, then you must have a *new* white post.

While this fact is true of inanimate things, it is also true of all human things in an even more special and frightful sense. The horrible rate at which human institutions grow old requires an almost unnaturally vigilant response from the citizen. It is the custom of casual romance novels and newspapers to say humanity suffers under old tyrannies. But, in reality, humanity has almost always suffered under *new* tyrannies—tyrannies that had meant freedom for the people barely twenty years before.

In this way, England was wildly joyful about the patriotic monarchy of Elizabeth, and then (almost immediately afterwards) was wildly angry about the trap of tyranny of Charles the First. So, again, in France the monarchy became intolerable to the people. And this happened not right after it had been simply tolerated, but right after it had been *adored*. The son of Louis the well-beloved was Louis the guillotined. Likewise, in nineteenth-century England the industrial manufacturer was entirely trusted as simply a champion of the people, until suddenly we heard the cry of the socialists that he was a tyrant eating the people like bread. And again, we have trusted the newspapers as the mouthpiece of public opinion. Only recently have some of us realized they are obviously nothing of the kind. Newspapers are, by nature, the hobbies of a few rich men.

We don't have any need to rebel against what is ancient; we must rebel against what is new. It is the new rulers–the capitalist and the editor–who control the modern world. There is no fear that a modern king will attempt to override the old constitution; it is more likely he will ignore the constitution and work behind its back. He will take no advantage of his ancient kingly power; it is more likely he will take advantage of his kingly powerlessness, of the fact that he is free from criticism and publicity. Because the king is the most private person of our time. It won't be necessary for anyone to fight anymore against censorship of the press. We don't need a censorship of the press. We have a censorship *by* the press.

This shocking rate at which popular human systems turn oppressive is the third fact in our perfect theory of progress. It must always be on the lookout for every privilege being abused, for every working right becoming a wrong. On this topic, I am completely on the side of the revolutionists. They really are right to be always doubtful of human institutions. They are right not to put their trust in princes or in any child of man. The chieftain, chosen to be the friend of the people, becomes the enemy of the people. The newspaper, created to

Beyond the Binary

In exploring Chesterton's ideas, you might initially label him a capitalist when reading his reservations about socialism, and then the next moment as a socialist when reading his thoughts on unrestrained capitalism. However, Chesterton defied these labels, identifying as neither a capitalist nor a socialist. Always a champion of family and community values, he waged a consistent battle against both Big Government and Big Business. His argument pivoted on the belief that concentrated wealth in capitalism and centralized control in socialism posed threats to individual freedom and human dignity. Chesterton's critiques of capitalism also delved into the impact on social relationships and the dehumanization stemming from excessive materialism. He writes, "It is Capitalism that has forced a moral feud and a commercial competition between the sexes; that has destroyed the influence of the parent in favor of the influence of the employer; that has driven men from their homes to look for jobs; that has forced them to live near their factories or their firms instead of near their families." Chesterton instead advocated for "distributism" – an alternative vision imagining a society where small property owners thrived, fostering a more equitable distribution of resources and power.

tell the truth, now exists to prevent the truth from being told.

Here, I felt I was really at last on the side of the revolutionary. And then I caught my breath again, because I remembered I was once again on the side of the orthodox. Christianity spoke again and said,

I have always asserted that men were natural backsliders, that human virtue naturally tended to rust or to rot. I have

always said that human beings go wrong, especially happy human beings, especially proud and prosperous human beings. This eternal revolution, this sense of suspicion that has sustained through the centuries, you (being a vague modern thinker) call the doctrine of progress. If you were a philosopher, you would call it the doctrine of original sin, as I do. You may call it cosmic progress as much as you like. I call it what it is— the Fall.

A Distrust of the Privileged

I have spoken of orthodoxy coming in like a sword; here I admit it came in like a battle-axe, because really (when I came to think of it) Christianity is the only thing left with any real right to question the power of those born and raised in privilege.

I have listened often enough to socialists who say the physical conditions in which the poor live ruins them and makes them mentally and morally inferior. I have listened to scientific people (and granted, there are still some scientific people not opposed to democracy) who say that if we give the poor healthier living conditions, vice and wrong will disappear. I have listened to them with a horrible attention, with a hideous fascination. It was like watching a man in a tree energetically sawing the branch he is sitting on. If these happy democrats could prove their case, they would strike democracy dead.

If the poor are utterly corrupted morally as these people say, then it may or may not be practical to allow them to vote. But it is certainly quite practical to deprive them of their vote. If the citizen with a bad bedroom can't cast a good vote, then the first and swiftest conclusion is that he should cast no vote. It would not be unreasonable for the governing class to say, "It may take us some time to reform his bedroom. But if he is the brute you say he is, it will take him very little time to ruin our country. Therefore, we will take your hint and not give him the chance."

I find it horribly amusing to watch the way in which the eager socialist diligently lays the foundation for the aristocracy he so strongly hates, blandly speaking at length about the evident inability of the poor to rule. It is like listening to someone at a dinner party apologizing for entering without evening attire, and explaining that he had recently been intoxicated, had a personal habit of taking off his clothes in the street, and had, on top of that, only just changed out of his prison uniform. We would feel at any moment the host might reply that really, if it was as bad as that, he shouldn't come in at all. Likewise, I listen to the ordinary socialist with a beaming face prove that the poor, after all of their experiences, can't really be trustworthy. At any moment, the rich may say, "Very well, then, we won't trust them," and then bang the door in his face.

Based on some recent views of genetics and environment, the case for placing power with aristocrats is quite overwhelming. If clean homes and clean air make clean souls, then why not give power (for the time being anyway) to those who undoubtedly have the clean air? If better conditions will make the poor more fit to govern themselves, why shouldn't better conditions already make the rich more fit to govern them? This ordinary environmental argument is fairly clear on the matter: the most comfortable class must lead us in Utopia.

Is there any answer to the proposition that those who have had the best opportunities will be our best guides? Is there any answer to the argument that those who have breathed clean air should decide for those who have breathed bad air? As far as I know, there is only one answer, and that answer is Christianity. Only the Christian Church can offer any rational objection to a complete confidence in the rich, because she has urged from the beginning that the danger was not in man's environment, but in man. And what's more, she has urged that as far as dangerous environments go, the most dangerous environment of all is the comfortable environment.

I realize that the most modern engineers have been quite busy trying to produce an abnormally large needle. And I know that the most recent biologists have been quite anxious to discover a very small camel. But if we shrink the camel to his smallest size or open the eye of the needle to its largest–if, in short, we assume the words of Christ to have meant the very least that they could mean, His words must at the very least mean this–that the rich are not very likely to be morally trustworthy.

Even watered-down Christianity is hot enough to boil all modern society to ashes. The smallest dose of the Church would be a deadly ultimatum to the world. Because the whole modern world is absolutely based on the assumption, not that the rich are necessary (which is reasonable), but that the rich are *trustworthy*, which (for a Christian) is not reasonable. You will hear for the rest of time, in all discussions about newspapers, companies, aristocracies, or party politics, this argument that the rich can't be bribed. The fact is, of course, that the rich man *is* bribed; he has been bribed already. That is why he is a rich man.

The whole case for Christianity is that anyone who is dependent upon the luxuries of this life is corrupt–spiritually corrupt, politically corrupt, financially corrupt. There is one thing that Christ and all the Christian saints have said with a sort of savage monotony. They have said simply that to be rich is to be in particular danger of moral wreck. It is not clearly un-Christian to kill the rich as violators of justice. And it is not clearly un-Christian to crown the rich as convenient rulers of society. It certainly is not un-Christian to rebel against the rich or to submit to the rich. But it is quite certainly un-Christian to *trust* the rich, to regard the rich as more morally safe than the poor.

A Christian may rightly say, "I respect that person's rank, even though he takes bribes." But a Christian cannot say, as all modern people are saying at lunch and breakfast, "a person of that rank would not take bribes," because it is a part of Christian belief that any person in any rank may take bribes. It is a part of Christian belief, but is also, coincidentally, an obvious part of human history. When people say a person "in that position" would be incorruptible, there is no need to bring up Christianity in order to refute it. Was Lord Bacon a shoe shiner when he accepted bribes? Was the Duke of Marlborough a chimney sweep? Even in the best Utopia, I must be prepared for the moral fall of any person in any position at any moment, and especially for my fall from my position at this moment.

Much vague and shallow journalism has been written to the effect that Christianity is similar to democracy, and most of it is hardly strong or clear enough to refute the fact that the two things have often fought. The real ground upon which Christianity and democracy are one is much deeper. The one uniquely un-Christian idea is the idea that the person who should rule is the person who feels they *can* rule. If everything else were Christian, this one thing would be heathen. If our faith comments on government at all, its comment must be this—that the person who *doesn't* think they can rule should rule. If the great paradox of Christianity means anything, it means this—that we must take the crown in our hands and go hunting in dry places and dark corners of the earth until we find the one person who feels they are unfit to wear it. The common idea here is wrong. We shouldn't crown the exceptional individual who knows they can rule. Instead, we must crown the much more exceptional individual who knows they can't.

Democracy versus Aristocracy

Now, here is one of the two or three essential defenses of democracy. The basic mechanics of voting is not democracy in and of itself, although currently it isn't easy to implement any simpler democratic method. But even the simple act of voting is profoundly Christian in this practical sense—it is an attempt to get at the opinion of those who would be too modest to offer it.

Voting is a mystical adventure. It is putting particular trust in those who do not trust themselves. That paradox is strictly unique to Christianity. There is nothing really humble about the self-denial of the Buddhist; the Hindu is mild, but he isn't meek. But there is something psychologically Christian about the idea of seeking for the opinion of the obscure rather than taking the obvious course of accepting the opinion of the prominent. To say that voting is particularly

Christian may seem somewhat curious. To say that canvassing or soliciting votes is Christian may seem quite crazy. But canvassing is very Christian in its primary idea. It is encouraging the humble. It is saying to the modest man, "Friend, go up higher." And if there is any slight fault in the perfectly holy act of canvassing, it would only be that canvassing may possibly encourage a lack of modesty in the canvasser.

Aristocracy is not an institution. Aristocracy is a sin, and generally a very socially acceptable one. It is simply the drift or slide of people into a sort of natural self-importance and praise of the powerful, which is the easiest and most obvious thing to do in the world. There are a hundred answers to this perversion of modern "power," one of which is that the fastest and boldest agencies are actually the most fragile and delicate. The swiftest things are the softest things. A bird is active because a bird is soft. A stone is helpless because a stone is hard. The stone can't help but go downward because hardness is weakness. The bird is able to go upwards because fragility is force. In perfect force there is a kind of lightheartedness, an airiness that can maintain itself in the air.

Modern investigators of the history of miracles have reluctantly admitted that a characteristic of the great saints is their power of "levitation." But they could take that even further. A characteristic of the great saints is their power of levity. Angels can fly because they take themselves lightly.

This has always been the instinct of the Church, and especially the instinct of Christian art. Remember how the Italian painter Fra Angelico represented all his angels, not only as birds, but almost as butterflies. Remember how the most earnest medieval art was full of light and fluttering draperies, of quick and playful feet. It was the one thing that the post-

Raphael painters could not imitate in the pre-Raphael painters. They could never recover the deep light-heartedness of
the Middle Ages. In the old Christian paintings, the sky over
every figure is like a blue or gold parachute. Every figure
seems ready to fly up and float about in the heavens. The tattered cloak of the beggar will raise him up like the rayed
plumes of the angels.

But the kings in their heavy gold and the proud in their
robes of purple will naturally sink downwards, because pride
can't rise to levity or levitation. Pride is the downward drag
of all things into an easy sense of dignity. It is easy to "settle
down" into a sort of selfish seriousness, but one has to rise to
a cheerful self-forgetfulness. A man "falls" into a brown office, but he reaches up at a blue sky. Seriousness is not a virtue. It would be heretical, although reasonable, to say that
seriousness is a vice. It really is a natural downward trend into
taking oneself seriously, because it is the easiest thing to do.
It is much easier to write a good *Times* leading article than a
good joke. Because seriousness flows out of people naturally,
but laughter is a leap. It is easy to be heavy, but hard to be
light. Satan fell by the force of gravity.

Now, it is the unique honor of Europe since it has been
Christianized that, while it has had aristocracy, it has always
at the back of its heart treated aristocracy as a weakness–generally as a weakness that must be allowed for. If anyone is
confused by this point, let them go outside Christianity into
some other philosophical atmosphere. Let them, for instance, compare the classes of Europe with the caste system
of India. This aristocracy is far more awful because it is far
more intellectual. It is seriously felt that the scale of classes
correlates to a scale of spiritual values–that the baker is better
than the butcher in an invisible and sacred sense.

But no version of Christianity, not even the most ignorant or perverse, ever suggested that a baron was better than a butcher in that sacred sense. No version of Christianity, however ignorant or extravagant, ever suggested that a duke could not be damned. I don't know, but in pagan society there may have been some serious division between the free man and the slave. But in Christian society we have always thought the gentleman to be a sort of joke, though I admit in some great crusades and councils he earned the right to be called a practical joke.

At the root of our souls, we in Europe never really took aristocracy seriously. It is only an occasional non-European foreigner who can even manage for a moment to take aristocracy seriously. It may simply be a patriotic bias (I don't think it is) but it seems to me that the English aristocracy is not only the epitome of aristocracy but is also the crown jewel of all actual aristocracies; it has all the virtues of oligarchies as well as all the flaws. It is casual, it is kind, it is courageous in obvious matters, but there is one great thing about it that overshadows even these. The best and most obvious quality of the English aristocracy is that nobody could possibly take it seriously.

Freedom to Bind

In short, I had created in my head slowly, as usual, the need for a law in Utopia. And, as usual, I found that Christianity had been there before me. The whole history of my Utopia has this same amusing sadness. I was always rushing out of my architectural office with blueprints for a new tower only to find it already there, shining in the sunlight and a thousand years old. For me, in many ways, God answered the prayer, "Go before us, O Lord, in all our doings."

In all humility, I really think there was a moment when I could have invented the institution of marriage out of my own head, but I discovered, with a sigh, that it had been invented already. But, since it would take too long to show how, fact by fact and inch by inch, my own conception of Utopia was only a copy of the New Jerusalem, I will take this one case of marriage as an example of the converging crash of all the other examples.

When ordinary opponents of socialism speak out against it, they argue that some desires of the socialists can't possibly be attained. But they always miss an important point. There are also some desires that frankly are not desirable. To wish that all men could live in equally beautiful houses is a dream that may or may not be attained. But to wish that all men should live in the *same* beautiful house is not a dream at all; it is a nightmare. To wish that a man should love all old women is an ideal that may not be attainable. But to wish that a man should regard all old women exactly as he regards his mother isn't only an unattainable ideal, but an ideal which shouldn't be attained.

I don't know if the reader agrees with me in these examples, but I will add the example which has made the most impact on me. I could never think of or tolerate any Utopia that didn't leave to me the freedom I care about most: the freedom to bind myself. Complete anarchy would not only make it impossible to have any discipline or faithfulness, but it would also make it impossible to have any fun.

To take an obvious example, it would not be worthwhile to bet if a bet were not binding. The termination of all contracts would not only ruin morality but also spoil sport. Now, betting and similar sports are only the stunted and twisted versions of the original instinct of humanity for adventure and romance, the instinct that has been talked about quite a bit in these pages. And these dangers, rewards, punishments, and fulfilments of an adventure must be real, or else the adventure is only a shifting and heartless nightmare. If I bet, I must be made to pay, or else there is no poetry in betting. If I challenge, I must be made to fight, or else there is no poetry in challenging. If I vow to be faithful, I must be cursed when I am unfaithful, or else there is no fun in vowing.

You couldn't even make a fairytale from the story of a man who was swallowed by a whale and then suddenly found himself at the top of the Eiffel Tower. Or of a man who was turned into a frog and then began to behave like a flamingo. The results must be real for even the wildest romance to have its intended effect; the results must be irrevocable. Christian marriage is the great example of a real and irrevocable result, and that is why it is the main subject of all our romantic writing.

This is my last example of the crucial things that I should ask of any social paradise–I should ask to be kept to my word, to have my oaths and agreements taken seriously; I should ask Utopia to avenge my honor on myself. All my modern Utopian friends look at each other hesitantly, because their greatest hope is the ending of all special ties. But again, I seem to hear, like a kind of echo, an answer from beyond the world:

You will have real obligations, and therefore real adventures when you get to my *Utopia. But the hardest obligation and the steepest adventure is to get there.*

8

The Romance of Orthodoxy

I often hear people complain about the hustle and bustle of our generation. But, in reality, the primary characteristic of our generation is a profound laziness, and the fact is that this real laziness is actually the cause of the apparent bustle. Let's take one obvious example. The streets are noisy with taxis and cars. This isn't due to human activity, however, but to human inactivity. There would be less bustle if there were more activity, if people were simply walking around. Our world would be more silent if it were more strenuous.

This truth applies not only to the apparent physical bustle, but also to the apparent bustle of the brain. Most of modern language exists only to reduce mental labor, and it saves mental labor much more than it should. Scientific phrases are used like scientific wheels and pistons to make the path of the comfortable even speedier and smoother. Long words go rattling by us like long railway trains. We know those trains carry thousands who are too tired or too apathetic to walk or think for themselves.

One thing I like to do is try to express any opinion of mine in only one-syllable words. If we say, "The social utility of the undefined sentence is recognized by all criminologists as a part of our sociological evolution toward a more human and scientific view of punishment," we could go on for hours with hardly a movement of the gray matter inside our skulls. But if we say, "I'd like Jones to go to jail and Brown to say when Jones should come out," we will discover, with a thrill of horror, that we are required to think. The long words are not the hard words. It is the short words that are hard. There is much more philosophical detail in the word "damn" than in the word "degeneration."

The New Theology

Long, comfortable words that save modern people the work of thinking are especially destructive and confusing in one particular way. The difficulty arises when the same long word is used in different situations to mean very different things. So, to take a well-known example, the word "idealist" has one meaning as it pertains to the philosophy of idealism and quite another as it pertains to someone with high ideals. In the same way, the scientific materialists have had good enough reason to complain about people mixing up "materialist" as a term of cosmic philosophy with "materialist" as someone who values material possessions. Likewise, to take a lesser example, the man who hates "progressives" in London always calls himself a "progressive" in South Africa, because the word means different things in two very different places.

The word "liberal" is just as confusing as it pertains to religion and as it pertains to politics and society. It is often said that all Liberals should be religion-rejecting freethinkers because they should love everything that is free. You might just as well say that all high idealists should be High Churchmen because they love everything that is high. You might as well say that Low Churchmen should like Low Mass, or that Broad Churchmen should like broad jokes. The thing is just semantics–simply an accident of words.

In actual modern Europe, a freethinker doesn't mean a man who thinks for himself. The word is used to mean a man who, having already thought for himself, has come to one particular class of conclusions: the material origin of the world, the impossibility of miracles, the improbability of personal immortality, and so on. And none of these ideas are particularly liberal or open-minded. In reality, almost all these ideas are definitely *illiberal*, and it is the purpose of this chapter to prove it.

In the following few pages, I will attempt to point out as quickly as possible that every single one of the things most strongly preached by liberalizers of theology would have a definitely illiberal effect on society. Almost every modern effort to bring freedom into the church is simply an effort to bring tyranny into the world. Because when people say they want to free the church, they don't mean freeing it in every way. They mean freeing it in a very specific way. They mean setting loose that specific set of dogmas called scientific–dogmas of monism, of pantheism, of Arianism, or of determinism. And every one of these (and we will take them one by one) can be shown to be the natural ally of oppression. In fact, it is quite remarkable (although less remarkable when you stop to think about it) that *most* things are the allies of oppression.

There is only one thing that can never go past a certain point in its alliance with oppression, and that is orthodoxy. Truthfully, it is possible for me to twist orthodoxy so that it could partly justify a tyrant. But I can easily make up a German philosophy to justify him entirely. Let's take in order these ideas that define the new theology of the modernist church.

The Case of Miracles

Let's take the most obvious example first—the case of miracles. For some extraordinary reason, there is this idea that it is more open-minded to disbelieve in miracles than to believe in them. Why this is, I can't imagine, nor can anyone tell me.

For some inconceivable reason, a "broad" or "liberal" Christian always means someone who wishes at least to reduce the number of miracles that have ever occurred; it never means someone who wishes to increase that number. It always means someone who is free to disbelieve that Christ came out of His grave; it never means someone who is free to believe their own aunt came out of her grave. It is common to find trouble in a parish because the parish priest can't admit St. Peter walked on water. But how rarely do we find trouble in a parish because the clergyman says his own father walked on the River Thames?

This isn't because (as the quick secularist debater would immediately say) miracles can't be believed in our time. It is not because "miracles don't happen." More supernatural things are purported to have happened in our time than would have been possible eighty years ago. Scientists believe in miracles much more than they did. Modern psychology is always discovering perplexing and even horrifying qualities of our minds and spirits. Miracles that older scientists frankly would have at least rejected are being asserted every hour by the new. The only thing that is still old-fashioned enough to reject miracles is the New Theology.

Truthfully, this idea that it is "freeing" to deny miracles has nothing to do with the evidence for or against them. It is simply a lifeless prejudice against the supernatural. The idea began not in the freedom of thought, but simply in the dogma of materialism. The man of the nineteenth century didn't disbelieve in the Resurrection because his liberal Christianity allowed him to doubt it. He disbelieved in the Resurrection because his very strict materialism didn't allow him to believe it. Lord Tennyson, a very typical nineteenth century person, uttered one of the instinctive truths of his time when he said there was faith in their honest doubt. There was indeed. Those words are profoundly true. In their doubt of miracles there was a faith in a fixed and even godless destiny—a deep and sincere faith in the incurable routine of the cosmos. The doubts of the agnostic were really only the dogmas of the materialist.

I will speak later of the facts and evidence of the supernatural. Here we are only concerned with this clear point: to the extent the liberal idea of freedom can be said to be on either side in this discussion about miracles, freedom is obviously on the side of miracles. Reform or (in the only tolerable sense of the word) progress means simply the gradual control of matter by mind. A miracle simply means the *swift* control of matter by mind. If you want to feed the people, you may think that feeding them miraculously in the wilderness is impossible, but you can't think it is not open-minded. If you really want poor children to visit the ocean, you can't think it is illiberal for them to go there on flying dragons, you can only think it is unlikely.

Liberalism simply means the liberty of man. A miracle simply means the liberty of God. You may thoughtfully deny either of these two things, but you can't call your denial a triumph of the liberal idea. The Church believed that man and God both had a sort of spiritual freedom. Calvinism took that freedom away from man but left it to God. Scientific materialism binds the Creator Himself. It leaves nothing free in the universe. And those who support this process are called the "liberal theologians."

This, as I say, is the lightest and most obvious case. The assumption that the doubt of miracles is somehow akin to open-mindedness or reform is literally the opposite of the truth. If a man can't believe in miracles, then that's the end of the matter; he is not particularly liberal, but he is perfectly honorable and logical, which are apparently much better things. But if he can believe in miracles, then he is certainly more liberal for it. Because miracles mean first, the freedom of the soul, and second, the soul's control over the tyranny of its environment.

Sometimes this truth is ignored in a particularly naïve way, even by the most capable people. For example, Bernard Shaw speaks with spirited old-fashioned disdain for the idea of miracles, as if they were a sort of betrayal of trust on the part of nature. He seems strangely unaware that miracles are only the final flowers on his own favorite tree, the doctrine of the all-powerful will. He calls our human desire for immortality a petty selfishness, forgetting that he has just called the desire for life a healthy and heroic selfishness. How can it be admirable to want to make your life infinite and yet terrible to want to make it immortal? No, if it is desirable for humanity to triumph over the cruelty of nature and routine, then miracles are certainly desirable. We will discuss later whether they are possible.

◉ An Unlikely Friendship ◉

G.K. Chesterton and George Bernard Shaw, two giants of the literary world in the early 20th century, shared a relationship marked by a blend of camaraderie and spirited disagreement. Despite their stark differences in ideology (and in body weight), the two maintained a deep and enduring friendship. And their debates, both in public and on paper, were not only a spectacle of intellect but also of witty banter. "I see there has been a famine in the land," Chesterton once joked, commenting on Shaw's rail-thin figure. "Yes, and I see the cause of it," he replied. This playful sparring that adorned their debates reminds us that even in disagreement, there is room for mutual respect and affection.

The Case of Buddhism and the Immanence of God

I must go on to the larger cases of this interesting mistake that the idea of "liberalizing" religion in some way helps the liberation of the world. The second example of it can be found in the question of pantheism, or rather of a certain modern philosophy called Immanentism–the common idea that God or some abstract force pervades and flows through everything. For many, this is often simply Buddhism. But this discussion is much more difficult, and I should approach it with more preparation.

The things said most confidently by smart people to crowded audiences are generally quite opposite to the truth. It is our widely held truths that are actually untrue. Here is an example. There is an overly simple sentiment uttered again and again at intellectual gatherings that goes like this: "The religions of the earth differ in rituals and ceremonies, but they are the same in what they teach."

This is false. It is the opposite of the truth. The religions of the earth don't differ greatly in rituals and ceremonies, but they do differ greatly in what they teach. It is as if a man were to say, "Don't be misled by the fact that *Christianity Today* and the *American Atheist* look entirely different, that one is painted on canvas and the other carved on marble, that one is triangular and the other hexagonal–read them and you will see they say the same thing."

The truth is, of course, that they are alike in everything except in the fact that they don't say the same thing. An atheist stockbroker in New York looks exactly like a Lutheran stockbroker in London. You could walk round and round them, studying them intently, without seeing anything particularly Lutheran in the hat or anything particularly godless in the umbrella. It is exactly in their souls that they are divided.

Likewise, the truth is that the difficult thing about all the different creeds of the earth is not as they say in this cheap statement–that they agree in meaning but differ in machinery. It is exactly the opposite. They agree in machinery, because almost every great religion on earth operates similarly–with priests, scriptures, altars, sworn brotherhoods, special feasts. They agree in the way of teaching; what they disagree about is the thing to be taught. Pagan optimists and Eastern pessimists both have temples, just as Republicans and Democrats both have newspapers. Creeds that exist to destroy each other both have scriptures, just as armies that exist to destroy each other both have guns.

The best example of this similarity between all human religions is the supposed spiritual similarity between Buddhism and Christianity. (Because they don't really mean *all* religions are the same. They generally avoid the ethics of most of the other creeds, except, of course, Confucianism, which they like because it isn't a religion. They are cautious in their praises of Islam, generally focusing only on its support for the poor. They rarely speak about the Muslim view of marriage, which there is quite a bit to be said about. And their attitude toward religious cannibals and fetish worshipers could even be called cold. But in the case of the great religion of Buddha, they sincerely feel a similarity to Christianity.)

Social scientists always insist that Christianity and Buddhism are very much alike—especially Buddhism. This is believed by many, and I believed it myself until I read a book giving the reasons for it. There were two kinds of reasons: resemblances that meant nothing because they were common to all humanity, and resemblances which weren't resemblances at all. The author of this book sincerely explained either that the two religions were alike in ways that all religions are alike, or else he described them as alike in ways in which they are quite obviously different.

So, as an example of the first kind, he said that both Christ and Buddha were called by the divine voice coming out of the sky (as if you would expect the divine voice to come out of the cellar). Or again, it was seriously urged that these two Eastern teachers, by a remarkable coincidence, both had to do with the washing of feet. You might as well say it was a remarkable coincidence that they both had feet to wash.

The other kind of similarities were those which simply weren't similar. For example, this reconciler of the two religions draws sincere attention to the fact that at certain religious feasts the robe of the Buddhist Lama is torn in pieces out of respect, and the remnants are highly valued. But this is the opposite of a resemblance because the garments of Christ were not torn in pieces out of respect, but out of mockery, and the remnants weren't highly valued except for what they would earn in the rag shops. It is almost like making the obvious connection between the two ceremonies of the sword: when it taps a man's shoulder and when it cuts off his head. It is not at all similar for the man.

These bits of silly detail really wouldn't matter much if it were not also true that these supposed philosophical similarities either prove too much or don't prove anything. The fact that Buddhism approves of mercy or of self-restraint is not to say it is especially like Christianity but is only to say that it isn't completely unlike all of human existence. Buddhists, in theory, disapprove of cruelty or overindulgence because all sane human beings, in theory, disapprove of cruelty or overindulgence. But to say that Buddhism and Christianity give the same philosophy about these things is simply false. All humanity does, in fact, agree that we are in a net of sin. And most of humanity agrees that there is some way out. But as to what is that way out, I don't think there are two institutions in the universe which contradict each other so absolutely as Buddhism and Christianity.

Even when I thought (with most other well-informed, unstudied people) that Buddhism and Christianity were alike, there was one thing about them that always confused me: the startling difference in their type of religious art. I don't mean in how it was represented technically, but in what they were clearly meant to represent. No two ideals could be more opposite than a Christian saint in a Gothic cathedral and a Buddhist saint in a Chinese temple. They are opposite in almost every way, but perhaps the clearest example of it is that the Buddhist saint always has his eyes shut, while the Christian saint always has them very wide open. The Buddhist saint has a sleek and balanced body, but his eyes are heavy and sealed with sleep. The medieval saint's body is wasted to its crazy bones, but his eyes are frightfully alive.

There can't be any real spiritual similarity between forces that produced symbols so different as that. It should be said that both images inherently are exaggerations or even perversions of their respective creeds, but it must be a real separation that could produce such opposite exaggerations. The Buddhist is looking with a particular intentness inward. The Christian is staring with a frantic intentness outward. If we continue to follow that clue, we will find some interesting things.

A short time ago, Annie Besant wrote an interesting essay announcing there was only one religion in the world, that all faiths were only versions or perversions of it, and that she was now prepared to say what it was. According to Besant this universal Church is simply the universal self. It is the doctrine that, in reality, we are all just one person, that there are no real walls of individuality between man and man. I could explain it this way–she doesn't tell us to love our neighbors, she tells us to *be* our neighbors.

That is Besant's thoughtful and evocative description of the religion that all people must agree upon. And I disagree more violently with this than anything I have ever heard in my life. I want to love my neighbor not because we are one, but precisely because we are *not* one. I want to adore the world, but not like I adore a mirror, because it is myself. I want to adore the world as a man loves a woman, because she is entirely different.

If souls are separate, then love is possible. If souls are united, love is obviously impossible. It might be said lightly that a woman loves herself, but she can hardly fall in love with herself, or, if she does, it must be a terribly boring love story. If the world is full of real individuals, then they can really be unselfish individuals. But according to Besant, the whole cosmos is only one enormously selfish person.

It is on this point that Buddhism is on the side of modern pantheism. And it's on this point that Christianity is on the side of humanity and liberty and love. Love desires personality; therefore, love desires division. It is natural for Christianity to be glad that God has broken the universe into little pieces, because they are *living* pieces. It is natural for Christianity to say, "little children love one another," instead of telling one large person to love himself.

This is the intellectual abyss between Buddhism and Christianity: for the Buddhist, personality is the fall of man, but for the Christian, personality is the purpose of God, the whole point of his cosmic idea. The world-soul of the Buddhist asks man to love it only so that he may throw himself into it. But the divine center of Christianity actually threw man out of it in order that he might love it. The oriental god is like a giant who has lost his leg or arm and is always seeking to find it. But the Christian God is like some giant who, being strangely generous, cut off his own right arm so that the severed limb might decide to shake hands with him.

We come back to the same tireless point regarding the nature of Christianity: all modern philosophies are chains that connect and bind, but Christianity is a sword that separates and sets free. No other philosophy makes God actually rejoice in the separation of the universe into living souls. But according to orthodox Christianity, this separation between God and man is sacred, because it is eternal. In order for a person to love God, it is necessary that there be not only a God to be loved, but a person to love him.

All those vague, modern minds for whom the universe is an immense melting-pot are exactly the minds which naturally shrink from that earthquake saying of our Gospels that declares the Son of God came not in peace but with a severing sword:

> *"Do not suppose that I have come to bring peace to the earth. I did not come to bring peace, but a sword. For I have come to turn 'a man against his father, a daughter against her mother, daughter-in-law against her mother-in-law—a man's enemies will be the members of his own household.'" (Matthew 10:34-35, NIV)*

The saying rings entirely true even considering what it obviously states, that anyone who preaches real love is bound to produce hate. It is as true of brotherly love as it is of divine love; fake love ends in compromise and common philosophy, but real love has always ended in bloodshed. But there is another, less obvious truth behind this utterance of our Lord. According to Himself, the Son was a sword separating brother and brother so that they would, for an age, hate each other. But the Father also was a sword, which in the black beginning separated brother and brother, so that these individuals could love each other at last.

This is the meaning of that almost insane happiness in the eyes of the medieval saint in the picture. This is the meaning of the sealed eyes of the Buddhist saint. The Christian saint is happy because he really has been cut off from the world; he is separate from things and is staring at them in astonishment. But why should the Buddhist saint be astonished at things? Since there is really only one thing, and as that thing is impersonal it can hardly be astonished at itself. The Buddhist can't feel a sense of wonder, because she can't praise God or praise anything as really distinct from herself.

Our primary concern here, however, is with the effect of this Christian admiration (an admiration that looks outward toward a deity distinct from the worshipper) on the general need for ethical behavior and social reform. And surely its effect is obvious enough. There is no real possibility of this idea of "oneness" producing any special impulse toward moral action. Because it naturally implies that one thing is as good as another, whereas action naturally implies that one thing is much better than another.

The English poet Swinburne, in the peak of his skepticism, tried in vain to wrestle with this. In "Songs before Sunrise," written under the inspiration of the Italian nationalist Garibaldi and the great unification of Italy, he proclaimed the newer religion and the purer God that should whither up all the priests of the world:

What doest thou now
Looking Godward to cry
I am I, thou art thou,
I am low, thou art high,
I am thou that thou seekest to find him,
Find thou but thyself,
Thou art I.

Now, the most immediate and obvious conclusion here is that tyrants are just as much the sons of God as Garibaldis, and that the terrible King Ferdinand II of Naples (having "found himself" with the utmost success) is identical with the ultimate good in all things. The truth is that the western energy that dethrones tyrants has been directly caused by the western theology that states, "I am I, thou art thou." The same spiritual separation that looked up and saw a good king in the universe looked up and saw a bad king in Naples. The worshippers of Ferdinand's god dethroned Ferdinand. The worshippers of Swinburne's god have covered Asia for centuries and have never dethroned a tyrant. The Indian saint may logically shut his eyes because he is looking at that which is I and Thou and We and They and It. It's a rational thing to do, but it isn't true in either theory or fact that it helps the Indian keep an eye on his British ruler.

That outward attentiveness which has always been the mark of Christianity (the command that we should *watch* and pray) has expressed itself both in typical western orthodoxy and in typical western politics. But both depend on the idea of a god that is transcendent, a deity that disappears. The most clever creeds may tell us to pursue God into deeper and deeper rings of the labyrinth of our own ego. But only we of Christianity have said that we should hunt God like an eagle upon the mountains–and we have killed all monsters in the chase.

So, we find here again that to the extent we value democracy and the self-renewing energies of the west, we are much more likely to find them in the old theology than in the new. If we want reform, we must cling to orthodoxy, especially in the matter of insisting on either the immanent god or the transcendent god. By emphasizing the immanence or permeance of God in all things, we get introspection, self-isolation, calm acceptance, social indifference–we get Tibet. By emphasizing the transcendence of God, we get wonder, curiosity, moral and political adventure, righteous anger–we get Christianity. By insisting that God is inside man, man is always inside himself. By insisting that God transcends man, man has transcended himself.

The Case of the Trinity

If we take any other doctrine that people call "old-fashioned," we will find the case to be the same. It is the same, for instance, in the deep matter of the Trinity. When we speak of the Unitarians, who deny the Trinity and assert a monotheistic God, it must never be without a special respect for their distinguished intellectual dignity and high intellectual honor. Unitarians are often reformers by the accident that throws so many small sects like them into a reformer's attitude. But there is nothing in the least liberal or similar to reform in the substitution of pure monotheism for the Trinity.

The complex God of the Athanasian Creed may be a puzzle for the intellect, but He is far less likely to display the mystery and cruelty of a Muslim Sultan than the lonely god of Mohammed. The god who is a simple, awful unit is not only a king but an Eastern king. The heart of humanity, especially of European humanity, is certainly much more satisfied by the strange symbol of the Trinity–the image of a council in which mercy pleads alongside justice, the idea of a sort of liberty and variety existing even in the innermost chamber of the world. Because Western religion has always eagerly felt the idea that "it is not good for man to be alone." This human tendency to be social asserted itself everywhere, as when the Eastern idea of reclusive hermits was practically expelled by the Western idea of social monks. In this way, even asceticism became brotherly, and the Trappist monks were sociable even when they were silent.

If this love of a living complexity is our test, then it is certainly healthier to have the Trinitarian religion than the Unitarian. Because for us Trinitarians (if I can say this with reverence)–for us God Himself is a society. It really is a fathomless mystery of theology, and even if I were theologian enough to take it head on, it wouldn't be relevant to do so here. It is sufficient to say here that this triple enigma is as comforting as wine and as open as an English fireside–that this mystery that bewilders the intellect utterly quiets the heart. But out of the desert, from the dry places and the dreadful suns, come the cruel children of the lonely God, the real Unitarians who with scimitar in hand have laid waste to the world. For it is not good for God to be alone.

The Case of the Danger of the Soul

The same rule of reform is true when discussing the danger of the soul, that difficult matter which has upset so many minds. It is crucial to hope for the eternal life of all souls, and it is quite reasonable to think that their salvation is inevitable, but it isn't particularly favorable to activity or progress. Our fighting and creative society should instead insist on the danger of everyone, on the fact that every person is hanging on by a thread or clinging to a cliff.

To say that all will be well no matter what is an understandable thing to say, but it can't be called the blast of a war trumpet. Europe should instead emphasize possible damnation, and Europe always has emphasized it. On this point, Europe's highest religion is in agreement with all its cheapest novels. To the Buddhist or the eastern fatalist, existence is a science or a plan which must end up in a certain way. But to a Christian, existence is a story which may end up in *any* way. In a thrilling novel (a purely Christian thing), the hero is not eaten by cannibals. But if the book is meant to be thrilling, it is essential that he *might* be eaten by cannibals. The hero (so to speak) must be an eatable hero. Likewise, Christian morals have not said that people will lose their soul but have always said that people must take care that they didn't. In short, Christian morals have said it is wicked to call a man "damned," but it is perfectly religious and philosophic to call him "damnable."

All the vast and shallow philosophies, all the huge systems of empty talk, go on about ages and evolutions and slow developments. But Christianity concentrates on the individual at the cross-roads. The true philosophy is concerned with the instant. Will a person take this road or that? –that is the only thing to think about, if you enjoy thinking. The eons are easy enough to think about. Anyone can think about them. The instant really is difficult, and our religion has intensely felt it. Because of this, our literature has dealt much with battle and our theology has dealt much with hell. The instant is full of danger, like an adventure book–it is at a life-threatening crisis. There is quite a bit of real similarity between popular fiction and Christianity. If you say that popular fiction is tasteless and gaudy, you only say what the boring and well-informed also say about the images in the Catholic churches.

According to the faith, life is very much like an adventure se-ries: life ends with the promise (or threat) "to be continued." And, with terrific indecency, life imitates the adventure book and ends at the exciting moment–because death is a distinctly exciting moment.

The point, however, is that a story is exciting because it contains such a strong element of will, of what theology calls *free* will. You can't finish a math problem however you want, but you can finish a story however you want. When someone discovered Differential Calculus, there was only one Differ-ential Calculus they could discover. But when Shakespeare killed Romeo, he might have married him to Juliet's old nurse if he had felt inclined. And Christianity has written such good literature exactly because it has insisted on the the-ological free will.

It is too large of a topic to be adequately discussed here, but what I have described is the main objection to that flood of modern talk about treating criminal behavior as a disease, about making a prison simply a hygienic environment like a hospital, of healing sin by slow scientific methods. What these people don't understand is that evil is a matter of active choice, whereas disease is not. If you say you are going to cure a habitual criminal just as you would cure an asthmatic, my brief and obvious answer is, "Show me the people who want to be asthmatic as badly as those who want to be criminals." A person may lie still and be cured of a disease. But she must not lie still if she wants to be cured of a sin. On the contrary, she must get up and jump around violently.

The whole point here is perfectly expressed in the very word we use for an individual in a hospital– "patient" is in the passive sense, and "sinner" is in the active. If a person is to be saved from influenza, he may be a patient. But if he is to be saved from stealing, he must be not a patient but an *im*patient. He must be personally impatient with thievery. All moral reform must start in the active will, not the passive.

Here again we reach the same substantial conclusion. To whatever extent we desire the definite reconstructions of our world and the dangerous revolutions which have distinguished and defined European civilization, we should not discourage the thought of possible ruin; instead, we should encourage it. If we want, like the Eastern saints, simply to contemplate how right things are, then of course we should only say that they will inevitably go right. But if we especially want to *make* them go right, we must insist that they may go wrong.

The Case of the Divinity of Christ

Lastly, this truth is yet again true in the case of the common modern attempts to diminish or to explain away the divinity of Christ. The fact may be true or it may not be. I will deal with that before I finish. But if the divinity is true, then it is without a doubt exceptionally revolutionary. The idea that a good man may have his back to the wall is nothing new to us, but the idea that *God* could have his back to the wall is a boast for all revolutionaries forever.

Christianity is the only religion on earth that has felt that omnipotence made God incomplete. Christianity alone has felt that God, to be completely God, must have been a rebel as well as a king. Christianity alone has added courage to the virtues of the Creator, because courage means that a soul passes a breaking point and does not break.

Now, in this I approach a dark and complex subject that isn't easy to discuss. I apologize in advance if anything I say here falls wrong or seems irreverent, as I am touching on a matter which the greatest saints and thinkers have understandably feared to approach. But that splendid story of the Passion of Christ distinctly suggests that the author of all things (in some unthinkable way) went not only through agony, but through doubt. It is written, "Thou shalt not tempt the Lord thy God." No, but the Lord thy God may tempt Himself, and it seems as if this is what happened in the garden of Gethsemane. In a garden Satan tempted man, and in a garden God tempted God. In some superhuman way, He experienced the human horror of pessimism. When the world shook and the sun was wiped out of heaven, it was not at the crucifixion, it was at the cry from the cross, the cry confessing that God had abandoned God.

And now let the rebels choose a creed and a god from all the gods of the world, carefully comparing all the gods of inevitable reincarnation and of unalterable power. They will not find another god who has himself been in rebellion. Now, (the subject grows too difficult for human speech) let even the atheists choose a god. They will find only one divine being who can relate to their isolation, only one religion in which God seemed for an instant to be an atheist.

The Mother of Reform and the Father of Confusion

All these things can be called the essential tenets of the old Christian orthodoxy. The main quality of this orthodoxy is that it is the natural source of revolution and reform, and the main flaw is that it is obviously only an abstract philosophy. Its main advantage is that it is the most adventurous and healthy of all theologies. Its main disadvantage is simply that it is a theology. It can always be critiqued by saying it is naturally theoretical and in the air. But it is not so high in the air to prevent great archers from spending their whole lives shooting arrows at it–yes, and their last arrows, too. There are people who will ruin themselves and ruin their civilization if they may also ruin this old fantastic tale.

This is the last and most astounding fact about this faith, that its enemies will use any weapon against it, whether it is the sword that cuts their own fingers or the fire that burns their own homes. People who begin to fight the Church for the sake of freedom and humanity end by throwing away freedom and humanity if only they may fight the Church. This is no exaggeration. I could fill a book with instances of this.

Mr. Blatchford set out as an ordinary Bible-smasher to prove that Adam was guiltless of sin against God. And in the midst of his arguing he admitted, as simply a side issue, that all the tyrants, from Emperor Nero to King Leopold, were guiltless of sin against humanity. I know a man who has such a passion for proving he will have no personal existence after death that he falls back on the position that he has no personal existence now. He calls on Buddhism and says all souls fade into one. In order to prove that he can't go to heaven he proves that he can't go to New Hampshire.

I have known people who protested against religious education with arguments against any and all education, saying that the child's mind must grow freely or that the old shouldn't teach the young. I have known people who showed that there could be no divine judgment by showing that there can be no human judgment, even for the most everyday purposes. They burned their own corn to set fire to the church; they smashed their own tools to smash orthodoxy. Any old stick was good enough to beat Christianity with, even if it was the last piece of wood from their own disassembled furniture.

There are religious fanatics who wreck this world for love of the other world. We certainly don't admire these people, and we hardly excuse them. But what are we to think about the fanatics who wreck this world out of hatred of the other? They sacrifice the very existence of humanity to the non-existence of God. These fanatics offer their victims not to any altar, but simply for the purpose of declaring the idleness of the altar and the emptiness of the throne. They are ready to abandon even the most basic desires by which all things live for the sake of their strange, eternal vengeance upon someone they think never even lived at all.

Yet this thing hangs in the heavens unhurt. Its opponents only succeed in destroying all that they themselves understandably hold dear. They do not destroy orthodoxy; they only destroy political courage and common sense. They do not prove that Adam was not responsible to God. How could they prove it? They only prove (based on their arguments) that the Czar is not responsible to Russia. They do not prove that Adam should not have been punished by God, they only prove that the nearest sweat-shop owner should not be punished by men. With their Buddhist doubts about personality they don't ensure that we have no personal life after we die, they only ensure that we don't have a very cheerful or complete one before we die. With their paralyzing idea that all our conclusions will turn out wrong, they do not tear the book of the Recording Angel, but they do make it a little harder to keep the books at Macy's.

Not only is the Christian faith the mother of all worldly revolution and reform, but its opponents are the fathers of all worldly confusion. The secularists have not wrecked sacred things, but the secularists have wrecked secular things, if that is any comfort to them. The Titans did not conquer heaven, but they laid waste to the world.

9

Authority and the Adventurer

The last chapter was concerned with the claim that ortho-doxy is not only (as we often hear) the only safe guardian of morality or order, but is also the only logical guardian of liberty, innovation, and advance. If our desire is to pull down the rich oppressor, we can't do it with the new doctrine of human perfectibility, but we can do it with the old doctrine of Original Sin. If we want to uproot deep cruelties or lift up lost people, we can't do it with the scientific theory of matter over mind; we can do it with the supernatural theory of mind over matter.

If we desire to really inspire people to keep watch and tirelessly tend to their lives, we can't do it by insisting on the Permeating God and the Inner Light, because these are at best reasons for contentment. But we can inspire people quite a bit by insisting on the transcendent God and the elusive light, because that means divine discontent. If we want to encourage the idea of a generous balance instead of a terrible dictatorship, then we will naturally be Trinitarian rather than Unitarian. If we desire European civilization to feel like a rescue mission, we should insist that souls are in real danger rather than that their danger is ultimately unreal.

If we wish to lift up the outcast and the crucified, we should want to think that an actual God was crucified rather than a simply wise man or hero. Above all, if we desire to protect the poor, we should be in favor of unchanging rules and clear dogmas. The rules of a club are sometimes in favor of the poor club members. But the simple drift of the club is always in favor of the rich one.

The Last Question

Now we come to the most important question which truly concludes the whole discussion. A reasonable agnostic, if he has happened to agree with me so far, may understandably turn right around and say,

You have found a practical philosophy in the doctrine of the Fall; very well. You have found a side of democracy that is dangerously neglected but wisely asserted in Original Sin; alright. You have found a truth in the doctrine of hell; I congratulate you. You are convinced that worshippers of a personal God look outwards and are progressive; I congratulate them. But even if we admit that those doctrines contain those truths, why can't you take the truths and leave the doctrines?

Let's say that all modern society trusts the rich too much because modern society does not understand the gravity of human weakness, and let's say that orthodoxy has a great advantage because (as it believes in the Fall) it does understand human weakness. Why, then, can't you simply understand hu-

man weakness without believing in the Fall? If you have discovered that the idea of damnation represents a healthy idea of danger, why can't you simply take the idea of danger and leave the idea of damnation? If you clearly see the seed of common sense in the nut of Christian orthodoxy, why can't you simply take the seed and leave the nut? To use that popular phrase of the newspapers which I, as a highly intellectual agnostic, am a little embarrassed to use, why can't you simply take what is good in Christianity, what you can define as valuable, what you can comprehend, and leave all the rest, all the definite dogmas that are inherently incomprehensible?

This is the real question, this is the last question, and it is a pleasure to try to answer it. The first answer is simply to say that I am a rational person. I like to have some intellectual justification as to why I think what I think. If I am treating man as a fallen being, then it is intellectually convenient to me to believe that he fell. And I also find, for some odd reason, that I can better deal with how a person uses her free will if I believe that she has it.

On this subject, however, I am even more rational. I don't intend to turn this book into one of ordinary Christian apologetics, although I would be happy to meet the opponents of Christianity in that more obvious arena. Here I am only describing my own journey in growing certain of spirituality. But I will pause to note that the more I saw of the simply vague arguments against the Christian philosophy, the less I was swayed by them. What I mean is that having found the moral philosophy of the Incarnation of Christ to be common sense, I then looked at the established intellectual arguments against the Incarnation and found them to be common nonsense.

In case my overall argument is criticized as lacking in ordinary apologetics, I will briefly summarize my own arguments and conclusions from a purely objective and scientific perspective. If I am asked, as a purely intellectual question, why I believe in Christianity, I can only answer, "For the same reason that an intelligent agnostic disbelieves in Christianity." I believe in it quite rationally based on evidence. But the evidence in my case, and also in the case of the intelligent agnostic, is not really in one, large piece of evidence. It is in an enormous accumulation of small but unanimous facts.

The secularist shouldn't be discredited because his objections to Christianity are miscellaneous and even untidy; it is precisely this untidy evidence that really convinces the mind. What I mean is that four books may not convince a man of a particular philosophy so much as one book, one battle, one countryside, and one old friend. The very fact that the things are of different kinds increases the importance of the fact that they all point to one conclusion. The non-Christianity of the average educated person today is almost always, to do them justice, made up of these loose but living experiences. I can't say that my kind of evidences for Christianity are any different than their vivid but varied evidences against it. Because when I look at all these different anti-Christian "truths," I simply discover that none of them are true. I discover that the true current and force of all the facts flows the other way. Let's look at some cases of this.

Three Anti-Christian "Truths"

Many sensible modern people have abandoned Christianity due to the combination of these three convictions.

First, that humans are simply another member of the animal kingdom as their shape, structure, and sexuality are, after all, very much like other animals. Second, that ancient religion rose up out of ignorance and fear. And third, that priests have infected societies with bitterness and gloom. Those three anti-Christian arguments are very different, but they are all quite logical, and they all point toward the same conclusion. The only objection to them that I have found is that they are all untrue.

If you quit looking at books about beasts and men and if you begin to actually look at beasts and men themselves, then (if you have any humor or imagination, any sense of the nonsensical) you will see that the surprising thing is not how similar the man is to the brute, but how *different* he is. It is the gigantic degree of divergence between the two that demands an explanation. The fact that humans and beasts are alike is, in a sense, obviously true. But the fact that such similar creatures can be so insanely unlike–that is what's so shocking and mysterious. The fact that an ape has hands is much less interesting to the philosopher than the fact that he does next to nothing with them. He doesn't play cards or the violin. He doesn't carve marble or carve meat.

Some people call old architecture barbaric and old art unsophisticated. But elephants don't build enormous temples of ivory even in a Baroque style; camels don't paint even *bad* pictures, despite the fact they are equipped with the material for many camel's-hair paint brushes. Certain modern dreamers say that ants and bees have a civilization that is superior to ours. Yes, they have a civilization, but that very fact only reminds us that it is an inferior civilization. Who has found an ant hill decorated with the statues of celebrated ants? Who has seen a beehive carved with the images of gorgeous queens of old?

No, the chasm between man and other creatures might be able to be explained without God, but it is still a chasm. We talk of wild animals, but man is the only wild animal. It is man that has broken free. All other animals are tame animals, keeping within the rugged bounds of their tribe or type. All other animals are domestic animals; man has always been undomestic, whether as a degenerate or a monk. So, this first superficial reason for materialism is, if anything, a reason against it. It is exactly where simple, natural biology leaves off that all religion begins.

I came to the same conclusion when examining the second of the three rationalist arguments, the argument that all we call divine began in ignorance and fear. When I attempted to examine this modern idea and its foundations, I simply found that there were no foundations. Science knows nothing whatsoever about pre-historic man for the spectacular reason that he is pre-historic. A few professors choose to guess that things such as human sacrifice were once approved and common and then they gradually dwindled, but there is no direct evidence of that, and the small amount of indirect evidence points in the other direction. In the earliest legends we have, such as the Biblical story of Isaac and the Greek story of Iphigenia, human sacrifice is not introduced as something old, but instead as something new, as a strange and scary exception to the rule demanded darkly by the gods.

History says nothing, and the legends all say the earth was much more kind in its earliest time. We can't find any tradition of progress, but the whole human race has a tradition of the Fall. As silly as it sounds, the historic popularity of this tradition of the Fall is actually used by some to disprove it. Educated people literally say this pre-historic disaster can't be true because every race of mankind remembers it. I simply can't keep up with these paradoxes.

Lastly, I came to the same conclusion regarding the third rationalist argument, the view that priests darken and embitter the world. I look at the world and simply discover that they don't. Those countries in Europe which are still influenced by priests are exactly the countries where there is still singing and dancing and colored dresses and art in the streets. It may be that Christian doctrine and discipline are walls, but they are the walls of a playground. The frame of Christianity is the only reason the pleasure of Paganism has survived.

Imagine if there were some children playing on the flat grassy top of some tall island in the sea. As long as there was a fence around the cliff's edge, they could throw themselves into any wild game and make the place the noisiest of nurseries. But imagine if we left and came back and the fence was knocked down, leaving the clear danger of the cliff. We would see that the children hadn't fallen over the side, but instead were all huddled in terror in the center of the island, and their song had ceased.

So, these three facts of experience which have convinced many agnostics are, from this perspective, turned completely around. I am left saying, "We need, then, an explanation for these Christian ideas: first, of the outstanding strangeness of humans amongst the animal kingdom; second, of the vast human tradition of some ancient happiness among humans; and third, of the survival of pagan joy inside the countries of the Church." One explanation, anyway, covers all three: the theory that the natural order of things was interrupted twice by some explosion or revelation that could only be described as otherworldly. Once, Heaven came down upon the earth in the form of a power called the image of God, by which man took command of Nature. And, when man had fallen short in empire after empire, Heaven once again came to save mankind in the awful shape of a man. This would explain why the masses always look backwards, and why the only corner where they in any sense look forwards is the little continent where Christ has His Church. But I don't want to assert my explanation here so much as the original remark that it explained. The ordinary unbelieving individual in the street is guided by three or four odd facts all pointing to something. I am guided by these facts, too, but when I came to look at the facts, I always found they pointed to something else.

Three More Anti-Christian "Truths"

I have given three of these ordinary anti-Christian arguments. If that isn't enough, I will give three more on the spur of the moment. The following are the kind of thoughts that when combined create the impression that Christianity is something weak and diseased. First, for instance, that Jesus was a gentle creature, sheepish and unworldly, a simply ineffective appeal to the world. Second, that Christianity arose and flourished in the dark ages of ignorance, and that the Church would like to drag us back to these times. And third, that the people still strongly religious or (so to speak) superstitious—such as the Irish—are weak, impractical, and behind the times.

I only mention these ideas to affirm what I have said all along, that when I looked into them independently, I found, not that the conclusions were unphilosophical, but simply that the facts were not facts. Instead of reading books about the New Testament, I read the New Testament. There I found a story not at all of a person with his hair parted in the middle or his hands clasped in prayer, but of an extraordinary being with lips of thunder and sensational decision–flinging down tables, casting out devils, escaping to the mountains with the wild secrecy of the wind, rallying the crowds in an almost frightful way. I found a being who often acted like an angry god–and always like a god.

Christ even had a way of speaking all to His own, not to be found, I think, anywhere else. It consists of an almost furious use of the *a fortiori*, which in Latin means a kind of argument that builds upon itself with clearer and more obvious examples of what was just stated. His "how much more" statements are piled one atop the other like castle upon castle in the clouds.

The things people have said *about* Christ have been, maybe wisely, sweet and submissive. But the things said *by* Christ are quite interestingly gigantesque; His speech is full of camels leaping through needles and mountains hurled into the sea. Morally speaking it is equally massive. He called Himself a sword of slaughter and told His followers to buy swords if they sold their coats for them. The fact that He used even wilder words when speaking of nonresistance only serves to greatly increase the mystery. But it also, if anything, somewhat increases the violence.

Calling a being like this insane can't explain it, because insanity is usually along one consistent path. The maniac is generally a mono-maniac. Here we should think back on the difficult definition of Christianity already given in chapter six: Christianity is a superhuman paradox of which two opposite passions may blaze beside each other. The one explanation of the Gospels that does explain Christ's behavior is that it is the mixed bag of one who from some supernatural height can see the bigger picture.

Now I will take the next idea that Christianity belongs to the Dark Ages. On this topic I wasn't content with reading modern commentaries. Instead, I read a little history. And in history I found that Christianity, rather than belonging to the Dark Ages, was the one path across the Dark Ages that wasn't dark. It was a shining bridge connecting two shining civilizations.

If anyone says that the faith arose in ignorance and savagery, the answer is simple: it didn't. It arose in the Mediterranean civilization in the highest peak of the Roman Empire. The world was swarming with skeptics and pantheism was as plain as the sun when Emperor Constantine – the first Roman emperor to embrace Christianity – nailed the cross to the mast. It is perfectly true that shortly after that the ship sank, but it is much more extraordinary that the ship came up again, repainted and glittering, with the cross still at the top.

This is the amazing thing the religion did–it turned a sunken ship into a submarine. The ark survived under the weight of the waters. After being buried under the debris of dynasties and clans, we arose and remembered Rome. If our faith had been simply a fad of the fading empire, then fad would have followed fad in those dark times. And if the civilization ever reemerged (and many civilizations like this have never reemerged) it would have been flying some new barbaric flag. But the Christian Church was the last life of the old civilization and the first life of the new. She took those who forgot how to build an arch and taught them to invent the Gothic arch.

In short, the most absurd thing that could be said of the Church is the thing we have all heard said of it. How can we say that the Church would like to bring us back into the Dark Ages? The Church was the only thing that ever brought us *out* of them.

The third in this second trinity of objections is a lazy claim taken from those who feel that people such as the Irish are weakened or paralyzed by superstition. I only added it because this is a peculiar case of a statement of fact that turns out to be a statement of falsehood.

It is constantly said of the Irish that they are impractical. But if we keep ourselves for a moment from looking at what is said about them and look at what they do, we will see that the Irish are not only practical, but quite painfully successful. The poverty of their country and the smallness of their numbers are simply the conditions under which they were asked to work. But no other group in the British Empire has done so much with so little. These people who we say are oppressed by priests are the only people of Great Britain who will not be oppressed by the rich. And when I looked at the character of actual Irishmen, I found the same thing. Irishmen are best at the especially hard professions–ironworking, law, and war.

In all these cases, then, I settled back on the same conclusions: the skeptic was quite right to go by the facts, except he hadn't looked at the facts. The skeptic is too gullible–he believes in newspapers or even in encyclopedias. Again, these three questions left me asking three more antagonistic questions. The average skeptic wanted to know how I explained the prissy tone in the Gospels, the connection of Christianity to medieval darkness, and the political impracticability of the Irish Christians. But I wanted to urgently ask right back, "What is this unparalleled power that first appeared in a man walking the earth like a living judgment–this power which can die with a dying civilization and force it to resurrect from the dead–this power which, last of all, can ignite a bankrupt population with a faith in justice so firm that they get what they ask, while others go away empty, so that the most helpless island of the British Empire can actually help itself?"

There is an answer, and it is to say that the power is truly from outside the world–that it is otherworldly, or at least caused by a real otherworldly disturbance. The great human civilizations, such as the old Egyptian or the current Chinese, deserve the highest gratitude and respect. Nevertheless, it isn't unfair for us to say that only modern Europe has constantly shown a power of self-renewal. It renews itself at the shortest intervals and all the way down to its smallest components. All other societies die finally and with dignity. We die daily. We are always being born again with almost obscene births.

I am not exaggerating when I say there is a sort of unnatural life in Christendom. It could be explained as a *supernatural* life. It could be explained as a frightful, monstrous life reviving what would have been a dead corpse. Because our civilization really should have died, by all sociological odds, in the apocalyptic Ragnarok of the end of Rome. You and I have no business being here at all. That is the weird cause of our situation. We have all returned from the dead; all living Christians are dead pagans walking about. Just as Europe was about to be gathered in silence to Assyria and Babylon, something entered into its body. And Europe has had a strange life—it is not too much to say that it has had the *jumps*—ever since.

The main point I am making here when dealing with all these common triads of doubt is to show that my own case for Christianity is rational, but it is not simple. It is an accumulation of varied facts, just like the attitude of the ordinary agnostic. But the ordinary agnostic has got his facts all wrong. He is a non-believer for a multitude of reasons, but they are untrue reasons. He doubts Christianity because the Middle Ages were barbaric, but they weren't. Because Darwinism is obvious, but it isn't. Because miracles don't happen, but they do. Because monks were lazy, but they were very diligent. Because nuns are unhappy, but they are particularly cheerful. Because Christian art was sad and bleak, but it was painted in particularly bright colors and glad with gold. Because modern science is moving away from the supernatural, but it isn't, it is moving toward the supernatural with the speed of a railway train.

A Democratic Belief in Miracles

Among these million facts all flowing in one direction there is, of course, one separate topic large enough to be briefly addressed by itself: the real experience of the supernatural. In chapter four I noted how wrong it is to assume the world must be impersonal because it is orderly, that a personal world is just as likely to desire order as it is to desire disorder. But I admit that, in a sense, my own conviction that a personal creation is more conceivable can't be debated. I won't call it a faith or a feeling because those words are mixed up with simple emotion. It is certainly an intellectual conviction, but it is an unprovable intellectual conviction, like my conviction that I am alive or that life is good. So, anyone who would like may call my belief in God simply mystical; the phrase isn't worth fighting about. But my belief that miracles have happened in human history is not a mystical belief at all. I believe in them based on the evidence just as I believe in the discovery of America.

There is a simple logical fact here that only needs to be stated and cleared up. Somehow or another an extraordinary idea has come about that those who don't believe in miracles consider the world evenly and fairly, while believers in miracles accept them only because of some rigid belief. But the fact is quite opposite to this. The believers in miracles accept them (rightly or wrongly) because they have evidence for them. The disbelievers in miracles deny them (rightly or wrongly) because they have a doctrine against them.

The open, obvious, democratic way to think is to believe an old lady when she bears testimony to a miracle, just as you would believe an old lady when she bears testimony to a murder. The simple, standard course of action is to trust the peasant's word about the ghost to the exact extent you trust the peasant's word about the landlord. As he is a peasant, he will probably have a great deal of healthy doubt about the existence of both. Still, you could fill the British Museum with evidence uttered by the peasant in favor of the ghost. If it comes to human testimony, you could drown in the flood of testimony in favor of the supernatural.

If you reject a ghost story, it can only be for one of two reasons. You reject the peasant's story either because the person is a peasant or because the story is a ghost story. To put it differently, you either deny the main principle of democracy, or you affirm the main principle of materialism–the total impossibility of miracles. You have every right to do so, but in that case *you* are the one holding the dogma. It is we Christians who respect the actual evidence. It is you rationalists who are constrained by your creed, refusing actual evidence. But I am not constrained by any creed on this topic, and as I have impartially investigated certain miracles of medieval and modern times, I have come to the conclusion that they happened.

Anyone who argues against these simple facts always argues in a circle. If I say, "Medieval documents confirm certain miracles as much as they confirm certain battles," they answer, "But medieval people were superstitious." If I then want to know how these people were superstitious, ultimately their only answer is that they believed in the miracles. If I say, "A peasant saw a ghost," I am told, "But peasants are so gullible." If I ask, "Why gullible?" the only answer is that they see ghosts. That's like claiming Iceland doesn't exist because only stupid sailors have seen it, and that the sailors are only stupid because they say they have seen Iceland.

It is only fair to add here that there is another argument the unbeliever could logically use against miracles, although the unbeliever generally forgets to use it. They may say that many of these stories of miracles were preceded by a preparation or acceptance of the spiritual on the part of the witness. In short, they say that a miracle could only come to those who believed in it. That may be true, but if it is true, how are we supposed to test it? If we are wondering whether certain results are caused by faith, it is pointless to repeat over and over that (if they happen) they are, indeed, caused by faith. If faith is one of the prerequisites for witnessing miracles, then those without faith have every right to laugh. But they have no right to judge. Being a believer may be, if it suits you, as bad as being a drunk. But still, if we were conducting a study on the inner workings of a drunkard's brain, it would be absurd to be always taunting him about having been drunk.

Let's say we were investigating whether men really see a red mist over their eyes when they are angry. Let's say sixty respectable citizens swore they had seen this crimson cloud. Surely it would be absurd to answer, "Oh, but you admit you were angry at the time." They could reasonably reply in a thunderous chorus, "How in the world could we discover, without being angry, whether angry people see red?" Likewise, the saints might rationally reply, "Let's say that the question is whether believers can see visions–even in this, if you are interested in studying visions it is pointless to object to studying believers." These people are still arguing in a circle–in that old, insane circle with which this book began.

The question of whether miracles ever happen is a question of common sense and of ordinary historical evidence, not of any conclusive scientific experiment. Some people talk about the need for "scientific conditions" when studying reports of spiritual phenomena, but surely we can dismiss this as idiotic. If we are asking whether a dead soul can communicate with a living soul, it is ridiculous to require this communication to take place under conditions in which not even two living souls in their right minds would seriously communicate with each other. The fact that ghosts prefer darkness doesn't disprove the existence of ghosts any more than the fact that lovers prefer darkness disproves the existence of love.

If you choose to say, "I will believe that Miss Brown called her husband a honey bear, or any other term of endearment, only if she will repeat it in front of seventeen psychologists," then I will reply, "Very well, if those are your conditions, you will never get the truth, because she certainly won't say it." It is just as unscientific as it is unphilosophical to be surprised that an insensitive environment doesn't produce certain extraordinary sensitivities. It is as if I said that I couldn't tell if there was a fog because the air wasn't clear enough, or as if I demanded perfect sunlight in order to see a solar eclipse.

So, as a commonsense conclusion, I conclude that miracles do happen. I am forced to the conclusion by a collaboration of facts: the fact that these people who encounter elves or angels are not the mystics or the dark dreamers, but instead fishermen, farmers, and all people common and cautious; the fact that we all know people who testify to spiritualistic incidents but are not spiritualists themselves; the fact that science itself admits these things more and more every day. Science will even admit the ascension of Christ if you call it "levitation," and will more than likely admit the resurrection when it has thought of another word for it. I suggest the word "revitalization."

The strongest fact of all, however, is the problem already mentioned, that these supernatural things can only be denied based on either anti-democracy or materialist dogma (we could even call it materialist mysticism). The skeptic always takes one of these two positions: either an ordinary man doesn't need to be believed or an extraordinary event must not be believed.

Now, I hope we can forget the other argument against miracles that people attempt–the simple statement that some of them are tricks or frauds by swindling fortune tellers and the like. That isn't an argument at all, good or bad. A fake ghost disproves the existence of ghosts just as much as a forged banknote disproves the existence of the Bank of England–if anything, it proves its existence.

Travelling Through a World of Spirits

So, given this belief that spiritual phenomena do occur based on evidence that is complex but logical, we then run into one of the worst mental evils of our age. The greatest disaster of the nineteenth century was that people began to use the word "spiritual" in the same way they used the word "good." They thought that to grow in sophistication and unearthliness was the same as to grow in virtue.

When the idea of scientific evolution was introduced, some feared it would encourage mere animality. It did worse. It encouraged mere *spirituality*. It taught people to think that so long as they were progressing from the ape they were going to the angel. But you can progress from the ape and go to the devil. We may be on the side of the angels, but we may also be on the side of the fallen angels–on the side of all the imperialism of the prince of the abyss, all arrogance and contempt for all obvious good.

Between this sunken pride and the towering humilities of heaven, there are, we must guess, spiritual things of different shapes and sizes. When we first encounter them, surely we make similar mistakes to those we would make if we went to a foreign continent and discovered new and various things. It would undoubtedly be hard at first to know what is superior and what is inferior. If a spirit came up from the underworld and visited any London street, that spirit wouldn't quite understand the idea of an ordinary horse and carriage.

He would guess that the carriage driver was a triumphant conqueror dragging behind him a kicking and imprisoned captive. Likewise, if we see spirits for the first time, we might mistake which is uppermost.

It isn't enough simply to find the gods; they are obvious. We must find God, the real chief of the gods. We must take a long, remarkable journey in supernatural phenomena in order to discover which are really natural. From this perspective I find the history of Christianity, and even the history of its Hebrew origins, quite practical and clear. It doesn't upset me to be told that the Hebrew god was only one of many gods. I know he was, without any research to tell me so. Jehovah and Baal looked equally important, just as the sun and the moon looked the same size. It takes time to learn that the sun is, without question, our master, and the small moon only our satellite.

So, given the belief that there is a world of spirits, I will walk in this world as I do in the world of men, looking for the thing that I like and think good. Just as I would seek clean water in a desert or work to make a comfortable fire at the North Pole, I will search the land of void and visions until I find something fresh like water and comforting like fire. I will search until I find some place in eternity where I am literally at home. And there is only one place like this to be found.

The Living Teacher

I have now said enough to show (to anyone who needed my explanation) that I have a basis for belief in the arena of ordinary, scientific apologetics. If we look at the facts (and look at them democratically and without contempt or bias) there is evidence first, that miracles happen, and second, that the most noble miracles belong to the Christian tradition. But I won't pretend this brief discussion is my real reason for accepting all of Christianity instead of taking the moral good out of it and leaving the rest, just as I could take it out of Confucianism. I have another much more solid and central reason for submitting to it as a faith instead of simply picking up tips from it as if it were a self-help scheme. And that reason is this.

The Christian Church in every practical way relates to my soul as a living teacher, not a dead one. It not only taught me yesterday but will almost certainly teach me tomorrow. I remember the day I suddenly saw the meaning of the shape of the cross; someday I may suddenly see the meaning of the shape of the mitre. One beautiful morning I saw why windows were pointed; some fine morning I may see why priests were shaven. Plato has told you a truth, but Plato is dead now. Shakespeare has shocked you with an image, but he won't shock you with any more. But imagine what it would be like to live with these men if they were still alive, to know that Plato might break out with an original lecture tomorrow, or that at any moment Shakespeare might shatter everything with a single song. The person who lives in contact with what they believe to be a living Church is a person always expecting to meet Plato and Shakespeare tomorrow at breakfast. They are always expecting to see some truth they have never seen before.

There is really only one illustration that works for this idea, and that is the parallel relationship in which we all began our lives. When your father told you, walking about the garden, that bees stung or that roses smelled sweet, you didn't think of taking the best out of his philosophy. When the bees stung you, you didn't call it an entertaining coincidence. When the rose smelled sweet you didn't say, "My father is a crude, barbaric symbol, preserving (maybe even unconsciously) the deep, delicate truths that flowers smell." No, you believed your father, because you had found him to be a living fountain of facts, a thing that really knew more than you, a thing that would tell you the truth tomorrow as well as today.

If this was true of your father, it was even truer of your mother–at least it was true of mine, the woman to whom this book is dedicated. Now, when society is in a rather useless uproar about the oppression of women, will no one say how much every man owes to the tyranny and privilege of women, to the fact that they alone rule education until education becomes pointless? Because a boy is only sent to be taught at school when it is too late to teach him anything. The real thing has been done already and thank God it is nearly always done by women. Every man is womanized simply by being born. They talk of the masculine woman, but every man is a feminized man. And if men ever march to protest this female privilege, I won't join their procession.

I clearly remember this fixed state of mind, that the very time when I was under a woman's authority the most, I was most full of passion and adventure. And I was most full because when my mother said that ants bit, they did bite. And because snow really did come in winter (as she said). Therefore, the whole world was a fairyland of wonderful fulfillments to me, and it was like living in the Old Testament, when prophecy after prophecy came true. I went out as a child into the garden, and it was a fascinating place to me, precisely because I knew its secrets. If I hadn't known anything about it, it wouldn't have been terrific, but tame. A wilderness with simply no meaning is not even impressive. But the garden of childhood was fascinating exactly because everything had a fixed meaning which could be found out at any moment. Inch by inch I might discover what was the use of the ugly shape called a rake or form some shadowy suspicion as to why my parents owned a cat.

So, since I have accepted Christianity as a mother and not simply as a random coincidence, I have again found Europe and the world to be like the little garden where I stared at the symbolic shapes of the cat and the rake; I look at everything with fresh eyes and anticipation. This or that ritual or doctrine may look as ugly and unusual as a rake, but I have found by experience that things like this end somehow in grass and flowers. A clergyman may be as apparently useless as a cat, but he is also as fascinating, because there must be some strange reason for his existence.

I will give one example out of a hundred. I don't feel any connection with that enthusiasm for sexual virginity which has certainly been an attitude of Christianity throughout history. But when I stop looking at myself and look at the world, I see that this enthusiasm is not only an attitude of Christianity, but also an attitude of Paganism and of high human nature across many spheres. The Greeks felt it when they carved the virgin goddess Artemis, the Romans when they clothed the virgin vestals, and the worst and wildest of the great Elizabethan playwrights clung to the literal purity of a woman as if they were clinging to the central pillar of the world. Above all, the modern world (even while mocking sexual innocence) has flung itself into a lavish worship of sexual innocence–the great modern worship of children. Because any person who loves children will agree that their unique beauty is damaged by even a hint of physical sex.

With all this human agreement, coupled with the Christian authority, I simply conclude that I am wrong, and the church is right. Or better yet that I am imperfect, while the church is universal. It takes all kinds of people to make a church; she doesn't ask me to be celibate. But I accept the fact that I have no appreciation for the celibates just as I accept the fact that I have no ear for music. The best human experience is against me on the subject of sex, just as it is against me on the subject of Bach. Celibacy is one flower in my father's garden, and he has yet to tell me its sweet or terrible name. But I may be told it one day.

In conclusion, this is my reason for accepting the religion and not simply the scattered and secular truths out of the religion: I do it because the thing hasn't simply told this truth or that truth, but instead has revealed itself as a truth-telling thing. All other philosophies say the things that seem to be obviously true; only this one philosophy has again and again said the thing that doesn't seem to be true, but is true. It is the only creed that is convincing where it is not attractive. It turns out to be right all along, like my father in the garden.

Buddhists, for instance, will preach an obviously attractive idea like reincarnation, but if we wait for what it logically causes, we will see the cruelty of the caste system and people behaving as if they are better than others. Because if people are beggars due to sins in a previous life, people will tend to despise beggars. But Christianity preaches some obviously unattractive ideas, such as original sin. But when we wait for what it causes, we see sympathy and brotherhood, and a thunder of laughter and pity, because only with the idea of original sin can we both pity the beggar and distrust the king.

Scientific people work to offer us better health; it is only later that we discover that by "health" what they really mean is bodily slavery and spiritual boredom. Orthodoxy makes us jump at the sudden brink of hell; it is only later that we realize that jumping is an athletic exercise highly beneficial to our health; it is only later that we realize that this danger is the root of all excitement and romance.

The strongest argument for God's grace is simply that it is ungracious. When we examine the unpopular parts of Christianity, we see they are, in reality, the pillars of the people holding them up. The outer ring of Christianity is a rigid wall of moral rules and professional priests. But inside that inhuman wall you will find the old human life dancing like children and drinking wine like men, because Christianity is the only protector of non-Christian freedom.

In the case of modern philosophy, however, it is the opposite. It is its outer ring that is obviously artistic and free. Its despair lies within. And its despair is that it doesn't really believe there is any meaning in the universe. Therefore, it can't hope to find any romance or adventure; its stories will have no storylines. A person can't expect any adventures in the land of anarchy, but a person can expect any number of adventures if they go travelling in the land of authority. They can find no meanings in a jungle of skepticism, but they will find more and more meanings when walking through a forest of doctrine and design. Here every moving thing has a story tied to its tail, like the tools or pictures in my father's house, because this world *is* my Father's house.

The Right Way Up

Now I end where I began—at the right end. I have entered, at last, the gate of a good philosophy. I have come into my second childhood. This larger and more adventurous Christian universe has one final feature that is difficult to express. Yet, as a conclusion to the whole matter, I will try to express it.

Any real argument about religion turns on the question of whether a human who was born upside down can tell when he comes right side up. The primary paradox of Christianity is that the ordinary condition a man is born into is not his sane or sensible condition, that in a way the normal state itself is abnormal. That is the core of the philosophy of the Fall. In Sir Oliver Lodge's interesting new Catechism, the first two questions are: "What are you?" and "What, then, is the meaning of the Fall of Man?" I remember entertaining myself by writing my own answers to those questions, but I soon found that they were very uncertain and agnostic answers. To the question, "What are you?" I could only answer, "God only knows." And to the question, "What is meant by the Fall?" I could sincerely answer, "That whatever I am, I am not myself."

This is the largest mystery of Christianity: something that we have never in any full sense experienced is not only better than ourselves but is even more natural to us than ourselves. And there is really no test of this except the simply experimental one that began this book, the test of whether something leads to sanity or insanity. It was only after I found orthodoxy that I found mental freedom. But, in conclusion, it is especially applicable to the ultimate idea of joy.

Some say that Paganism is a religion of joy and Christianity is a religion of sorrow. It would be just as easy to prove that Paganism is pure sorrow and Christianity pure joy. These comparisons mean nothing and take us nowhere. Everything human must have in it both joy and sorrow. The only interesting point is how the two things are balanced or divided. And the really interesting thing is this, that the pagan was (for the most part) happier and happier as she approached the earth, but sadder and sadder as she approached the heavens. The cheerfulness of the best Paganism, such as the playfulness of the poets Catullus or Theocritus, is, to be sure, an eternal cheerfulness that should never be forgotten by a grateful humanity. But all of it is a cheerfulness about the facts of life, not about the origin of life.

To the pagan, the little things are as sweet as the small brooks breaking out of the mountain, but the big things are as bitter as the sea. When the pagan looks at the very core of the cosmos, he is struck cold. Behind his gods, who are simply tyrannical, sit the three Fates, who are deadly. No, the Fates are worse than deadly–they are dead. And when rationalists say the ancient world was more enlightened than the Christian, from their point of view they are right. Because when they say "enlightened," they really mean darkened with hopeless despair.

It is deeply true that the ancient world was more modern than the Christian world. The common bond is that the ancients and the moderns have both been miserable about existence, about everything, while Christian medievals were happy about that at least. But if the whole thing pivots on our attitude toward the cosmos, then there was more cosmic contentment in the narrow and bloody streets of Florence than in the pagan theaters or open gardens of Greece. The

Italian painter Giotto lived in a gloomier town than the Greek philosopher Euripides, but he lived in a happier universe.

Most people have been forced to be happy about the little things, but sad about the big things. Nevertheless (and I offer this last dogma defiantly), it isn't natural for humans to be like this. Man is more himself, man is more manlike, when joy is the fundamental thing in him, and grief is only surface level. Sadness should be an innocent intermission, a tender and fleeting state of mind; praise should be the permanent pulsation of the soul. Pessimism is at best a short break for our emotions; joy is the boisterous labor by which all things live. Yet, according to the pagan or the agnostic, this primary human need can never be fulfilled. Joy ought to expand to fit the universe, but for the agnostic it must shrink and cling to one corner of the world. Grief ought to be condensed, but for the agnostic its emptiness spreads throughout an unthinkable eternity.

This is what I call being born upside down. It would be true to say the agnostics are topsy-turvy because their feet are dancing upwards in meaningless bliss, while their brains are in the abyss. To the modern man, the heavens are actually below the earth. The explanation is simple here: they are standing on their heads, which is a particularly weak pedestal to stand on. But when they have found their feet again, they know it.

Christianity satisfies suddenly and perfectly the ancient human instinct for being the right way up. The creed satisfies it completely because by it joy becomes something gigantic and sadness something special and small. The space above us is not deaf due to a mindless universe; the silence is not the heartless silence of an endless and aimless world. Instead, the silence around us is a small and pitiful stillness, like the immediate stillness in a hospital room. Perhaps bad things are allowed as a sort of mercy to us, because the frantic energy of divine things would knock us down like drunken horseplay. We can take our own tears more lightly than we could take the great light-heartedness of the angels. So maybe we sit in a starry chamber of silence, while the laughter of the heavens is too loud for us to hear. Joy, which was the small promotion of the pagan, is the gigantic secret of the Christian.

As I end this chaotic book, I open again the strange, small book from which all Christianity came, and I am haunted by how much it confirms this idea. The tremendous Christ which fills the Gospels towers in this respect, as He does in every other, above all the thinkers who ever thought they were tall. His sadness was natural, almost casual. The Stoics, both ancient and modern, were proud of holding back their tears. He never held back His tears; He showed them plainly on His open face at any common sight, such as the far sight of His native city. Yet He did hold something back. Serious supermen and professional politicians are proud of restraining their anger. He never restrained His anger. He flung furniture down the front steps of the Temple, and asked people how they expected to escape the damnation of Hell. Yet He did restrain something.

I say this with reverence; in that stunning personality there was something that must be called shyness. There was something that He hid from everyone when He went up a mountain to pray. There was something that He covered constantly by abrupt silence or impulsive isolation. There was some one thing that was too great for God to show us when He walked upon our earth. And I sometimes like to think it was His mirth.

THANK YOU FOR READING

If you enjoyed the book, please consider leaving a review by scanning the code to the right. We really appreciate every review we get. It only takes a few seconds, and each one helps us reach more people!

ABOUT THE EDITOR

Peter Northcutt is known for making difficult things simple, first as a youth pastor, then as a Teach for America corps member, and now as the creator of Modern Saints. He lives in Calvert City, Kentucky with his beautiful wife and son.

Go to modernsaints.com to read more of his work.